Stories of Transformative Learning

INTERNATIONAL ISSUES IN ADULT EDUCATION

Volume 14

Scope:
This international book series attempts to do justice to adult education as an ever expanding field. It is intended to be internationally inclusive and attract writers and readers from different parts of the world. It also attempts to cover many of the areas that feature prominently in this amorphous field. It is a series that seeks to underline the global dimensions of adult education, covering a whole range of perspectives. In this regard, the series seeks to fill in an international void by providing a book series that complements the many journals, professional and academic, that exist in the area. The scope would be broad enough to comprise such issues as 'Adult Education in specific regional contexts', 'Adult Education in the Arab world', 'Participatory Action Research and Adult Education', 'Adult Education and Participatory Citizenship', 'Adult Education and the World Social Forum', 'Adult Education and Disability', 'Adult Education and the Elderly', 'Adult Education in Prisons', 'Adult Education, Work and Livelihoods', 'Adult Education and Migration', 'The Education of Older Adults', 'Southern Perspectives on Adult Education', 'Adult Education and Progressive Social Movements', 'Popular Education in Latin America and Beyond', 'Eastern European perspectives on Adult Education', 'An anti-Racist Agenda in Adult Education', 'Postcolonial perspectives on Adult Education', 'Adult Education and Indigenous Movements', 'Adult Education and Small States'. There is also room for single country studies of Adult Education provided that a market for such a study is guaranteed.

Stories of Transformative Learning

Michael Kroth
University of Idaho Boise, USA

and

Patricia Cranton
University of New Brunswick, Canada

SENSE PUBLISHERS
ROTTERDAM/BOSTON/TAIPEI

A C.I.P. record for this book is available from the Library of Congress.

ISBN: 978-94-6209-789-6 (paperback)
ISBN: 978-94-6209-790-2 (hardback)
ISBN: 978-94-6209-791-9 (e-book)

Published by: Sense Publishers,
P.O. Box 21858,
3001 AW Rotterdam,
The Netherlands
https://www.sensepublishers.com/

Printed on acid-free paper
Cover photograph by Patricia Cranton

To adult educators, storytellers all, who engage in transformative learning daily.

TABLE OF CONTENTS

ACKNOWLEDGEMENTS

We would like to thank Peter de Liefde from Sense Publishers for his support throughout this entire project. He embraced this book from the time we first proposed it to him. He and his colleagues have greatly facilitated the process of producing and publishing this book, which has been a boon for us as we both work with demanding schedules. We are especially grateful to Jolanda Karada, who has shepherded us through the production process with great skill.

We deeply appreciate the time and effort contributed by the storytellers in the book. Without them, obviously, there would be no book. They have been more than informative and illustrative; they have been and continue to be inspiring. By sharing their lives they will help many understand not only transformative learning but also life. We are most grateful for the storytellers who contributed to this book. Art, Susan, Alyssa, Laurence, Nayoung, Olutoyin, Mike, Kelly, Libby, and Jose—this book would not exist without you. Thank you.

From Michael Kroth

I thank those who, through their example, love, friendship, and wisdom teach and inspire me daily. In particular, I am grateful for my wife, children, all my family and dear friends who encouraged and supported me through this and many other life projects. The older I get the more I realize the importance of relationships in my life. I especially value Patricia Cranton, from whom I have learned so much as we created this book, not only about transformative learning and book writing, but about life. I am a better writer, thinker, scholar, and person because I have had the good fortune to work with her.

From Patricia Cranton

I thank Jack Mezirow who influenced my life tremendously through his writing and his support of my writing. I thank the many students and colleagues who taught me how to listen to and tell stories. I especially thank my colleague Michael Kroth who has helped me to be a better collaborator.

I thank my family, all of whom have four legs and wear fur coats, even in the summer. They sacrificed walks and were patient about delayed afternoon snacks. They danced at the sound of the computer's closing tune each day.

PREFACE

Transformative learning theory was originally based on a research study of women returning to college as reentry students (Mezirow, 1975). At that time, it was called perspective transformation, and it was a stage-based, largely rational description of how these women experienced a transition in their lives. The stages began with the disorienting experience of going back to school, and included steps related to self-examination, critical reflection, feelings of alienation, relating to others sharing the same experience, exploring options, building self-confidence, acquiring new knowledge and skills, and reintegrating into society with revised perspectives. Although Mezirow was criticized immediately, and continually during the decades that followed, about being "too rational" and "ignoring context," it can be seen even in the list of the original phases, that Mezirow incorporated participants' feelings and the context in which the transformation occurred.

It was almost 20 years before Mezirow (1991) introduced transformative learning as a comprehensive theory of adult learning. At this time, he drew on variety of diverse disciplines such as social philosophy (Habermas, 1971), psychoanalysis, and social activism (Freire, 1971). In spite of his interdisciplinary approach, the same critiques continued, and, indeed, Mezirow welcomed these critiques and used them to enhance his theory (Mezirow, 2000). The updated comprehensive theory was based on constructivist assumptions—where meaning is constructed by individuals in social contexts and is validated through communication with others. The understanding of experience is filtered through meaning perspectives (later called "habits of mind") which include individuals' uncritically assimilated perspectives. When a person encounters an experience which calls his or her meaning perspectives into question, this can lead to critical reflection and critical questioning of the perspectives. Mezirow (2000) sees discourse as central to the process of exploring options to potentially invalid meaning perspectives (this relates back to his 1975 phase of relating to others who share the same experience). The reflection and discourse may or may not lead to transformation; there are many circumstances that can prevent the change in perspective from taking place.

In the years that followed Mezirow's presentation of transformative learning theory, several scholars responded with alternative perspectives, based on the critiques of the original work. John Dirkx, for example, focused on an extrarational approach that included intuitive and emotional ways of knowing (Dirkx, 2001, 2012). O'Sullivan (2003, 2012) presented a broad vision of transformative learning that spanned relational, societal, and global perspectives. Belenky and Stanton (2000) described transformative learning in terms of relational processes.

Cranton and Taylor (2012) propose the need for developing a unified theory of transformative learning; that is, a theory in which the cognitive and rationale perspective, the extrarational perspective, the emphasis on social change, and

xiii

the relational approach can all peacefully co-exist. Cranton and Taylor suggest that bringing these perspectives together and integrating them can strengthen the theory and make it more relevant to those individuals who work toward fostering transformative learning.

The literature that addresses how transformative learning is fostered (for example, Cranton, 2006; Mezirow & Taylor, 2009) focuses on the creation of a climate that is conducive to critical questioning and the deliberate presentation of points of view that are contradictory with each other or discrepant with the views of the participants or both. Discourse or dialogue is generally considered to be an essential component of fostering transformative learning, as are opportunities for critical self-reflection or activities to encourage reflection (journals, role-playing, debates, arts-based activities, and the like). Educators also often work with transformative learning experiences that occur outside of the classroom by bringing them into the classroom for discussion.

Storytelling is one way in which educators and learners can understand the process of transformative learning through first-hand accounts of others' transformative experiences. Telling stories, reading others' stories, and reading fiction all serve the purpose of exposing learners to alternative perspectives, a process that is at the heart of critical reflection and critical self-reflection, which is, in turn, central to transformative learning.

Stories illustrate the process of recognizing that we are positioned within a particular culture with certain privileges and power relations that we can often recognize better in the stories we hear from others rather than in the stories we tell ourselves. This recognition can lead to reflection and in turn to the questioning of previously unchallenged values and assumptions.

Jarvis (2006) uses stories in the form of reading fiction to encourage "particular kinds of transformation" (p. 76). She suggests that reading fiction can offer disorienting dilemmas, encourage dialogue where contradictions can emerge, lead to imagining alternatives, and allow for the trying on of different points of view, all of which are facets of transformative learning. Jarvis derives her ideas from research she conducted in a college classroom using popular romantic fiction. Her participants were women from different ethnic and social backgrounds and women of different ages, who were preparing for entry into higher education. We suggest that telling stories and reading others' non-fictional stories has the same potential.

The adult educator who has a goal of creating an environment that is conducive to transformative learning is interested in fostering healthier, more open, permeable, and better justified assumptions about the world. When an individual is hurt by events in the world, he or she may have a tendency to withdraw and lose trust. Adult educators can help people to test all the reasons behind unhealthy personal strategies and build agency instead of helplessness. In other words, when the events people experience hit them hard, as will be illustrated in the stories in this volume, readers will be able to see what educators can do in response.

The stories are not intended to be used as a "tool," but rather they are the medium through which readers can understand how adult educators and individual adult learners can promote transformative learning in a wide range of situations – suggesting the universality of the principles and practices available to both learners and educators.

PURPOSE

The purpose of *Stories of Transformative Learning* is to encourage people to explore the potential for transformative learning in their own lives, practices, and communities. Our goal is not to present a "how to" manual for encouraging transformative learning; there are no recipes or strategies that can ensure transformative learning occurs in any context (Mezirow, 1991). In fact, it is potentially unethical to assume that we can "change" others' beliefs and assumptions (Mezirow, 1991). Instead, what we hope to do is to illustrate the transformative learning process through stories of how individuals have engaged in the process both inside and outside of the classroom. There are at least two ways that educators, learners, and others in helping professions can make use of this approach: one is to set up an environment in a classroom, workshop, or other venue where people are exposed to alternative perspectives through stories; another is to bring stories of transformative learning occurring in real life contexts into classroom and group discussions.

We hope to increase readers' sense of agency and hope for better and more self-directed, self-fulfilling lives. By demonstrating in a very personal way how others have examined and reconsidered hidden assumptions that constrained the quality and potential of their lives, we will give readers hope that they may do the same.

NEED

There have been many accounts of transformative learning experiences. However, missing in the literature are first-hand stories from the individuals who have personally experienced transformative learning either in formal classrooms or in everyday life. We believe stories told directly, unconstrained by scholarly citations and abstract interpretation, are more likely to resonate with readers and to inspire people to create the conditions where transformative learning can occur in their lives and professional practice.

INTENDED AUDIENCES

The primary audiences for this book are adult educators and adult learners. Transformative learning can occur in any situation where adults learn—in formal settings, informal settings, and in independent, autodidactic settings. It may be the case that adult educators want to incorporate storytelling into their courses but, just as likely, educators want to draw on stories that happen outside of their classroom and bring them into the course in a variety of ways, depending on the subject area. Adult learners who are not being led directly led by an adult educator professional—people who engage in individual and independent learning projects, what Candy (1991) describes as autodidaxy—will also find this book to be useful and informative.

A second, and related, audience is those involved in professional development activities. These include human resource development professionals, faculty development, and others involved in training and development activities. They are professionals working in organizations, K-12 and higher education, and areas such as medical education and nursing education.

The third audience is the group of people who are just interested in reading good, engaging, non-fiction stories. This book is filled with short, biographical memoirs that may appeal to a particular group of readers who are interested in individual success stories that also lead to positive societal consequences.

CONTENT

The book opens with setting out the case for making a difference through fostering transformative learning. Chapter 1 includes an overview of transformative learning, with an emphasis on the development of a unified theory of transformation, as called for by Cranton and Taylor (2012), and especially what this means for practitioners of adult education. The chapter establishes the groundwork for the stories that follow and gives a rationale for how we, as practitioners, can foster transformative learning so as to make a difference for individuals, organizations, and society.

In the second chapter, storytelling is introduced as a way of understanding self and society in general. There are several approaches to storytelling in the literature ranging from Rossiter and Clark's (2009) concept of narrative learning, through Tyler and Swartz's (2012) and Boje's (2007) use of storytelling in organizations. We do not engage in a detailed theoretical discussion here, but rather introduce the readers to how we understand ourselves, our experiences, our identities, and the world we live in through stories.

These two strands are pulled together in Chapter 3, as we discuss transformative learning through storytelling. In doing this, we demonstrate how transformative learning takes place through the reading and writing of stories. Chapters 4 through 8 relay stories from adult educators and learners about their transformative experiences. These stories illustrate the process of transformative learning, the context in which it took place, and the role of the educator and others in fostering transformative learning. We have grouped these stories into the following categories: psychological dilemmas, loss and trauma, educational experiences, social change, and spirituality.

In Chapter 9, we discuss and interpret the stories, and in Chapter 10, we provide a summary of what we learned about practice, research, and theory from our storytellers.

ABOUT THE AUTHORS

Michael Kroth is an Associate Professor at the University of Idaho in Adult/ Organizational Learning and Leadership and is a recipient of the university's Hoffman Award in Teaching Excellence. He has written or co-authored four books, including *Transforming Work: The Five Keys to Achieving Trust, Commitment, and Passion in the Workplace* (with Patricia Boverie), *The Manager as Motivator*, and *Career Development Basics* (with McKay Christensen). *Managing the Mobile Workforce: Leading, Building, and Sustaining Virtual Teams*, co-authored with David Clemons, is his latest book.

Patricia Cranton is a retired Professor of Adult Education, currently affiliated with the University of New Brunswick in Canada and Teachers College at Columbia University. She has been Professor of Adult Education at Penn State University at Harrisburg, St. Francis Xavier University, University of New Brunswick, and Brock University in Canada, and Associate Professor at McGill University. Patricia Cranton's recent books include *Planning Instruction for Adult Learners* (3rd edition, 2012), *Becoming an Authentic Teacher* (2001), *Finding our Way: A Guide for Adult Educators* (2003), *Understanding and Promoting Transformative Learning* (2nd edition, 2006), and *A Guide to Research for Educators and Trainers of Adults* (3rd edition, 2014) with Sharan Merriam as second author. Patricia was the co-editor of *The Handbook of Transformative Learning* (2012, with Ed Taylor). Patricia has edited five New Directions in Adult and Continuing Education volumes, most recently *Authenticity in Teaching* (2006) and *Reaching out across the Border: Canadian Perspectives in Adult Education* (with Leona English as co-editor, 2009). Patricia has taught courses in the area of transformative learning since 1994. She was inducted into the International Hall of Fame for Adult and Continuing Education in 2014.

Michael Kroth, Boise, Idaho, United States
Patricia Cranton, New Brunswick, Canada
May, 2014

ABOUT THE STORYTELLERS

Ten people share their stories in this book. How they were chosen is described in Chapter Nine. They come from different walks of life. Each of the stories is told in the person's own words, with only light editing from us. We gave them the options of using pseudonyms, their first names only, full names, or their full names and affiliations. They made the choices of what to include for their name and affiliation. Each is accomplished in her or his unique way as the stories demonstrate.

CHAPTER 1

FOSTERING TRANSFORMATIVE LEARNING

To transform something...is to cause a metamorphosis in form or structure, a change in the very condition or nature of a thing, a change into another substance, a radical change in outward form or inner character, as when a frog is transformed into a prince or a carriage maker into an auto factory.

James M. Burns, *Transforming Leadership*, p. 24

When we are children, growing up in a family, community, and culture, we absorb the values and beliefs we encounter in our surroundings. We believe that our parents and teachers know best, and we strive to please those important people in our lives by following their values and beliefs. In turn, parents, teachers, and others strive to instill their values and beliefs in young people, believing these are the best way to guide them. Of course, this does not necessarily hold true in circumstances where young people are oppressed, abused, or neglected, but on the whole, children uncritically assimilate the values and perspectives that are modeled by the adults they trust and believe in.

Starting in adolescence, young people come to a developmental stage where they need to differentiate themselves from their family and sometimes their community and culture. Mainly, they are looking for their own identity as separate from that of their parents. Jung (1971) calls this process individuation. Individuation, though, is not a one-time stage of development; it continues through the lifespan. Individuation, says Jung, is the process of separating oneself from the collective of humanity and reintegrating with humanity with a new understanding of who we are and where we have been. It includes bringing the unconscious into consciousness, and understanding our anima or animus, the masculine and feminine facets of personality. It is a life goal to define one's self as both separate from and as a part of humanity.

In adulthood, people continue to acquire new knowledge and skills and to elaborate on the knowledge and skills they have already acquired, but they also engage in revisions to that knowledge, and perhaps mostly importantly, to their values, beliefs, and assumptions. Mezirow (2000) distinguishes between four kinds of learning: the acquisition of new knowledge and skills, the elaboration on existing knowledge and skills, the revision of meaning schemes (beliefs and values), and the revision of meaning perspectives (a larger view of the world). This is where transformative learning comes in.

1

When a person has a firmly entrenched set of values and beliefs, often absorbed in childhood, it can take a lot for that person to be willing to question them. Perhaps most often, people simply are not willing to engage in that questioning. But when they encounter an event that challenges their values or beliefs and their expectations of what will happen next, a disorienting dilemma as Mezirow (2000) says, they can be nudged into that questioning process. This can be the beginning of transformative learning. A disorienting dilemma can be, for example, the death of a loved one, the loss of a job, a move from one culture to another, or any major life transition, positive or negatively perceived (Cranton & Taylor, 2012b). A disorienting dilemma can also be created deliberately in a more formal learning environment such as a course, workshop, or retreat, by exposing learners to alternative perspectives through reading, film, fiction, and discussion.

MAKING A DIFFERENCE

Adult educators are concerned about making a difference in the lives of students. Educators at all levels share this goal, but adult educators are more likely to be helping individuals to transform their previously uncritically assimilated perspectives, and educators of young people are more likely to be engaged in the formation rather than the transformation of values, preferences, beliefs and assumptions. Storytelling is a universal human activity. We see storytelling everywhere—in songs, in fiction, in memoirs, in painting, in music and in theatre. People love to tell their stories. We find, in our teaching, that when we invite students to "tell a story" about their experiences or to relate "their story" to a theoretical concept, the learning is much more meaningful than if the discussion stays on an academic and detached level. In our online teaching, for example, where learning relies on discussion, students sometimes feel that they need to include academic references in their posts, but once they are freed from that expectation their stories become so much more meaningful and interesting. Both the storytellers and the readers of the stories are drawn into each others' experiences and learn from them; this learning has the potential to be transformative.

In this chapter, we set out the case for making a difference through fostering transformative learning. The chapter includes an overview of transformative learning theory, with an emphasis on moving toward a unified or integrated theory of transformation, as called for by Cranton and Taylor (2012a), and especially what this means for practitioners of adult education. The chapter establishes the groundwork for the stories that follow and gives a strong rationale for how we, as practitioners, can foster transformative learning so as to make a difference for individuals, organizations, and society.

OVERVIEW OF TRANSFORMATIVE LEARNING THEORY

Transformative learning has been defined by Mezirow and others from the beginning as leading to a deep shift in perspective during which habits of mind become more open, more permeable, more discriminating, and better justified (Cranton, 2006; Mezirow, 2000). According to Mezirow, the process centers on critical reflection and critical self-reflection, but other theorists (for example, Dirkx, 2001) place imagination, intuition, and emotion at the heart of transformation. Generally, transformative learning occurs when a person encounters a perspective that is at odds with his or her current perspective. This discrepant perspective can be ignored, or it can lead to an examination of previously held beliefs, values, and assumptions. When the latter is the case, the potential for transformative learning exists, though it does not occur until the individual changes in noticeable ways. This overview draws on Cranton and Taylor's (2012b) chapter in the *International Handbook of Learning*.

Mezirow's (1975) development of a theory of transformative learning began when his wife, Edie, returned to college as an adult. Her experience led Mezirow to contemplate the changes that women returning to college might experience (Edie sometimes laughingly claims credit for the initial exploration of transformative learning theory). In the context of the women's movement of the time, Mezirow decided to study women returning to college as adults. In general, he found that the experience led the women to question and revise their personal beliefs and values in a fairly linear ten-step process. They questioned, for example, why some women were expected to be home to make meals for their husband, but others were not. Mezirow described the results of his study in a ten-phase description. At this time he called the developing theory as "perspective transformation." The ten steps of perspective transformation were:

- Experiencing a disorienting dilemma (they encountered beliefs that were different from the beliefs they held)
- Undergoing a self-examination (they were led to question their own beliefs)
- Feeling a sense of alienation from traditional social expectations (the women felt isolated and alienated)
- Relating their discontent to similar experiences of others (they recognized that their situation was shared by others)
- Exploring options for new ways of acting (the women contemplated, "what now?")
- Building competence and self-confidence in new roles (they realized that they needed to gain new skills and new roles)
- Planning a course of action (building competence and confidence led to a plan to make changes in their lives)
- Acquiring the knowledge and skills for implementing a new course of action (developing a plan for change often led to the need for further knowledge and skills)
- Trying out new roles and assessing them (the women tried out the new roles and contemplated how well they suited what they wanted to do)
- Reintegrating into society with the new perspective (the women brought their new learning and their changed perspectives back into their everyday life in society)

Not much attention was paid to Mezirow's original study, except for a few critiques in which he was chastised for neglecting the social context (the women's movement) of the time. But 15 years later, Mezirow (1990) edited a book on fostering critical reflection in adulthood, which was really a book of strategies and methods for facilitating transformative learning. And in the next year, he published his comprehensive theory of transformative learning in his book, *Transformative Dimensions of Adult Learning* (Mezirow, 1991). At this time, he made certain to give his work credibility, and one way he did this was to draw on the work of Habermas (1971), a German social philosopher who proposed that there were three kinds of human interests that led to three kinds of knowledge—instrumental (technical), practical (communicative), and emancipatory. In this framework, transformative learning is emancipatory knowledge. The critics did not give up, and Mezirow's book was challenged on the basis of his "misinterpretation" of Habermas, but eventually, this philosophical foundation of his work was accepted.

Mezirow (1991) also described three types of meaning perspectives—epistemic (about knowledge and how we obtain knowledge), sociolinguistic (understanding ourselves and social world through language), and psychological (concerned with our perception of ourselves largely based on childhood experiences). He suggested that people absorb each of these types of meaning perspectives from their family, community, and culture. The perspectives are deeply embedded and largely unquestioned until the individual encounters a dilemma that brings this to his or her attention.

As a part of his theory development Mezirow (1991, 2000) created a structure to explain the process of transformative learning. In 1991, Mezirow's structure involved meaning schemes (assumptions, beliefs, and values) and meaning perspectives (a web of meaning schemes that formed a larger world view. In 2000, his terminology changed somewhat. He defined a "frame of reference"as including the assumptions, beliefs, and expectations that influence a person's behavior. "Habits of mind" and "points of view" replaced "meaning perspectives" and "meaning schemes." A habit of mind is a set of assumptions that acts as a lens or a filter for understanding experience (similar to a meaning perspective). A habit of mind is expressed as a point of view and is a cluster of meaning schemes—specific expectations of what people see and how they see it. For example, if I (Patricia) believe that men should not control the finances of their women partners, I may chastise my granddaughter when she tells me her boyfriend is controlling her money. Habits of mind or frames of reference are like grooves in the mind—the way we automatically think, feel, and act without question or further thought. Habits of mind, since they are deeply embedded, are difficult to articulate, let alone question.

Frames of reference act as filters or a lens for interpreting experience. When I interact with my granddaughter, I interpret her decisions about how to manage her finances using my lens related to the roles of women and men and partnership. When an individual comes upon a new experience, it either reinforces the frame of reference or gradually stretches its boundaries, depending on how it conforms to prior experience. However, when an individual has a radically different or incongruent experience (for example, the death of a loved one or moving to a different country), where the experience cannot be assimilated into the frame of reference, it is either rejected or there is a development of new frame of reference—a perspective transformation.

Mezirow emphasizes rational and cognitive transformative learning, but other theorists include different processes. Mezirow was critiqued for originally explaining transformative learning primarily as a cognitive process, and his later views are more inclusive of other perspectives, such as the role of emotions in the process. Dirkx (2001), for example, substitutes imagination, intuition, and emotion for critical reflection. Dirkx (2001, 2006) draws on the Jungian concept of individuation to describe transformative learning as an imaginative, intuitive, emotional, and soulful experience (the way of mythos rather than logos). Mythos is a facet of knowing that engages symbols, images, stories, and myths, paying attention to the small everyday occurrences of life and listening to individual and collective psyches. Dirkx (2006) suggests that the experience of emotional dynamics in learning come from "largely unconscious issues evoked by various aspects of the learning setting, such as the self, designated leaders, other learners, the context in which learning occurs, and the task that is the explicit focus of our learning" (p. 17). Individuation, suggests Dirkx, is mediated through emotion-laden images (p. 18). This gives us quite a different take on the process of transformative learning.

Dirkx was informed by the earlier work of Boyd and Myers (1988, Boyd, 1985, Boyd, 1989, Boyd, 1991) who called on Jungian psychology to explain transformative learning. Discernment, rather than reflection, is the central process of transformation in this perspective; symbols, images, and archetypes lead to personal enlightenment as people bring the unconscious to consciousness. Boyd (1989) emphasizes the role of small groups in working with unconscious content. The group becomes the archetypical "mother" and influences the way in which people in the group create images and work through personal dilemmas. Boyd (1989) defines transformation as "a fundamental change in one's personality involving conjointly the resolution of a personal dilemma and the expansion of consciousness resulting in greater personality integration" (p. 459). This goes back to a belief that individuation is central to transformative learning, as mentioned at the beginning of the chapter. In the extrarational perspective on transformative learning, people bring the unconscious into consciousness through imagination, intuition, and emotional experiences. We enter into a conscious relationship with images as we discover who we are as separate from and the same as others. As Dirkx (2006) puts it, "Conscious participation in this process directs our psychic energy toward creative, life-enhancing, constructive, and potentially transformative activities" (p. 19).

Following a different path, psychologists such as Kegan (2000) and Tennant (2012) take a developmental view of transformative learning. From this point of view, transformative learning describes shifts in the way people make meaning—moving from a simplistic reliance on authority to more complex ways of knowing or higher orders or consciousness. Belenky and Stanton (2000) report on a similar progression, but they emphasize connected knowing (through collaboration and acceptance of others' views rather than autonomous, independent knowing).

Transformative learning theory has long been critiqued for neglecting social change, and this critique is especially focused on Mezirow's writing even though he draws on the works of Freire and Habermas, both of whom have social change as a central goal. But Mezirow sees transformative learning as a *learning process,* and a learning process is an individual undertaking, even though it may have social consequences or be fueled by social change. At the same time, though, social change has long been a goal of adult education, including the Antigonish Movement in Canada in the 1920s, where ordinary people were helped to develop economic independence and the Highland Folk School in the US in the 1930s where the development of literacy skills was seen to be a way to foster both social and personal transformation.

In general, the process of transformative learning is consistent with what is known as constructivism. Constructivism is a view of learning where the learner is an active participant in the learning process, not a passive recipient, creating and interpreting knowledge rooted in personal experience. That is, people "construct" meaning from their own experiences, and different people view the same event in different ways. Learners use their personal experiences in order to interpret their current learning. So, for example, I may respond to a change in my work environment based on my prior understandings of how my work environment affects my daily life. If I encounter a supervisor who is authoritarian in her approach to working with her staff, and if I have negative feelings about authoritarian leadership, I may well respond to this particular supervisor based on my prior experience. Based on the assumption that there are no fixed truths, or at least none that we can fully understand, and that change is continuous, individuals cannot always be confident of what they know or believe, and therefore they need to find different and better ways to understand their world. Mezirow (2000) argues that adults have a need to better understand "how to negotiate and act upon our own purposes, values, feelings and meanings rather than those we have uncritically assimilated from others—to gain greater control over all lives as socially responsible clear thinking decision makers" (p. 8).

Toward a Unified Theory of Transformative Learning

Good theory can stimulate a number of research threads that often lead to promising theoretical inquiry, and it is a normal process for scholars to build upon and to develop initial theory into something more comprehensive and deeper. A powerful and enduring theory builds upon and integrates relevant lines of inquiry. As we can already see, transformative learning theory has spawned a range of theorizing and research since it was originally proposed. Dirkx (2001) has said that "transformative learning represents one of the most generative ideas for both practitioners and researchers concerned with adult learning" (p. 139). Mezirow's original conceptualization has benefitted from increasing depth, lines of inquiry, and perspectives. Taking what has been learned and moving to a more unified, integrated theory seems timely. In spite of earlier calls to take a more integrative view of the theory (for example, Cranton & Roy, 2003; Cranton, Dirkx & Mezirow, 2005), the research and literature still remains divided. Most of the research uses Mezirow's perspective as a theoretical framework. But Gunnlaugson (2008) describes "first wave" and "second wave" theories of transformative learning, the first wave being those works that build on, critique, or depart from Mezirow's seminal work, and the second wave being those authors who work towards integrative, holistic, and integral perspectives. There are still only a few articles that could be described as being in the "second wave."

Since the late 1990s, transformative learning theory has been described in relation to at least three categories: a cognitive rational approach, an extrarational approach, and a social change approach. But the number of categories grew over time. In 2008, Taylor listed the following: a psychocritical perspective (including Mezirow's cognitive and rational approach); a psychoanalytical approach (including Dirkx and others who describe individuation as transformative learning); a psychodevelopmental perspective (viewing transformative learning across the lifespan); a social emancipatory perspective (helping oppressed people develop a critical consciousness); a neurobiological perspective (based on brain research using medical techniques); a cultural-spiritual perspective (grounded in a culturally relevant and spirituality understanding of transformation); a race-centric view (in which people of African descent are the "subjects" of the transformative experience (p. 9); and a planetary view (in which the goal is the reorganization of the whole system—political, social, and educational). Taylor distinguishes between perspectives that have the individual as the "unit of analysis," with little consideration being given to the social context, and those perspectives that focus on social change (for example, the social emancipatory approach) where, presumably, individuals are not the "unit of analysis."

It is valuable, of course, to understand the different strands of theory development, especially in a field as new as transformative learning theory, but classification systems can paralyze rather than stimulate the thinking about transformative learning. And where do we go from here, beyond further categorization? As transformative learning theory is in its third decade of development, it seems that we can move toward putting these pieces back together in a meaningful way—a way that will help practitioners and researchers get on with their work.

The ways scholars might move toward considering theory integration might take different forms. Our point here is not to suggest the means to conceptually integrate the diverse strands of inquiry but that it is a timely endeavor. Therefore, in this book, we move toward the unified and integrated perspective proposed by Cranton and Taylor (2012a).

There is no reason that both the individual and the social perspectives cannot peacefully coexist; one does not deny the existence of the other, but rather they share common characteristics and can inform each other. Similarly, people are both intuitive and cognitively oriented. Some people focus on relationships and values;

and sometimes the process is developmental. Different individuals may experience the same event in quite different ways. Also the same individual may experience different events in different ways. It is our intent in this book to rely on a unified or integrated theory of transformative learning and to illustrate the various facets of that learning through the stories people tell.

Michael's story illustrates a transformative learning experience that is in progress and illustrates an integrative approach to questioning and reflecting.

Michael: I am writing this while sitting in my apartment in Torino, Italy. I turned 61 the day I flew here three months ago, and I return to Idaho in just a week. I am teaching here as part of a studies abroad program. My wife joined me for part of this journey but though I had briefly met a couple of people here I really knew no one when I arrived in Italy. I deliberately put myself in a situation where I would be totally immersed in another culture, situation, and a language I did not know.

Why? Partly for the adventure, of course, and to learn about the art, culture, history and the people of this country, a place I have wanted to explore for many years, but mostly to explore myself. I am just a tad past a later-in-life tenure and promotion process, both my parents have died within the last two or so years, and I have had two recent heart surgeries. I have felt lately as if I were on a thoughtless treadmill and that I was ceding my ability to choose my life because of quotidian activity traps. My lack of intention was allowing the situation and not me to dominate my life. Time was moving forward. Planning for my future was not.

To put a point on it, I have been struggling with how to make the most—in every way—of this next phase of my life. I didn't want to waste it by going through the motions of heading to retirement age. So I sought out this opportunity for self-reflection and learning.

But once here the insights did not come. I was enraptured by the frescoes of Raphael, touched by the bravery of martyrs and heretics, and moved by stories of heroic leadership. I engaged myself in learning Italian and practicing it whenever I could. There is something intimately humbling about being so helpless that you don't even know how to order a cup of coffee without asking for assistance.

With the usually-solid moorings of relationship, language, and domicile cast aside, it might seem easy to set also adrift the constraints to thinking as well. Not so for me. As the date of return approached I realized that the journey had been enriching and transforming but not epiphanal. The trip had not reset my sails.

Then, just days ago a friend mentioned an opportunity for learning that I had not even considered before, and as I thought about it pieces started falling into place and over the last day or so the next phase of my career has been like a jigsaw puzzle picture emerging from the fragments.

It is very early in the transformative learning process for me, and I do not know where this will lead if anywhere, but I intend to reflect upon this, seek additional insight and information and, depending on where that takes me, to try some stuff out. Regardless, this has given me more depth of knowledge about myself and about what is meaningful to me at this stage in life.

What a Unified or Integrated Theory Means for Adult Education Practitioners

At the risk of over-simplifying, a theory from an interpretive perspective has two main purposes: (1) to describe observations of a phenomenon in a way that makes sense of the observations and organizes them into patterns, and (2) to guide practice. A good educational theory should help practitioners with their practice. Practitioners might find it difficult to apply eight or more seemingly unrelated or even conflicting theoretical perspectives related to the same phenomenon. If, however, an adult educator realizes that different individuals may engage in transformative learning in different ways, or the same individual may engage in transformative learning differently depending on the content and context of the process, then the practitioner can set up an environment and select strategies in such a way that they would be supportive of all possibilities.

In other words, a unified theory of transformative learning would allow educators to draw on those aspects of the theory that fit with their context and their goals. For example, an adult literacy educator may draw on a social emancipatory perspective along with a psychocritical perspective. A trainer working in an organizational context, where the acquisition of skills is the primary goal, may choose to support critical thinking and critical reflection so that the possibility of technical learning spiraling into emancipatory learning exists. A teacher in a graduate adult education program may set up readings, discussions, and a variety of resources that are relevant to individuals' styles and preferences as well as the content and context of the program.

In order to frame practice with an integrative theory of transformative learning, an expanded definition of transformative learning is called for. We began our overview with the following definition: "Transformative learning is a deep shift in perspective during which habits of mind become more open, more permeable, more discriminating, and better justified." This definition is open enough to accommodate the processes discussed here, but we could make this clearer and more explicit.

Transformative learning is a process by which individuals engage in the cognitive processes of critical reflection and self-reflection, intuitive and imaginative explorations of their psyche and spirituality, and developmental changes leading to a deep shift in perspective and habits of mind that are more open, permeable, discriminating, and better justified. Individual change may lead to social change, and social change may promote individual change.

From another perspective, it is interesting that Mezirow's ten phases, listed above, still incorporate all the theorizing we have just described. Phase one, experiencing disorienting dilemmas, (encountering beliefs different from ones they held), might include a range of beliefs about psyche, spirituality, philosophy, science, and so on. Phase two, self-examination, might include critical reflection, discernment, or other processes which scholars have yet to discover or describe. This simple list remains a useful way to look at a unified transformative learning process for adult practitioners in the field.

Transformative learning can occur with the help and support of educators, counselors, coaches, and other helping professionals, or it can occur informally in individuals' lives, often without being recognized or named as transformative learning. When educators deliberately foster transformative learning, there is one central facet to this process, regardless of context—learners are introduced, in some way, to points of view that are potentially discrepant to the points of view they hold. It is this discrepancy between what can be and what is that leads to critical reflection, exploration, questioning, and possibly a shift in perspective.

As we know, there are many ways that this discrepancy can be created or discovered (see, for example, Cranton, 2006). Journals, role plays, critical incidents, debates, questioning, experiential activities, films, and thought-provoking readings all have the potential for setting up the circumstances that are conducive to transformative learning. In recent years, attention has turned to arts-based strategies, narrative learning, and storytelling (Jarvis, 2012, Lawrence, 2012, Rossiter & Clark, 2007). In this book, we are especially interested in the telling and reading of real-life stories (in other words, storytelling and narrative learning). In the next section, we provide an overview of the role of storytelling and narrative learning in fostering transformative learning. We return to this topic in more detail in Chapter 2.

The Role of Storytelling and Narrative Learning in Fostering Transformative Learning

Rossiter and Clark (2007) provide an excellent overview of narrative learning and narrative knowing with a focus on the practicalities of facilitating narrative learning in the classroom. Clark and Rossiter (2008) describe the essential features of narrative learning: hearing stories, telling stories, and recognizing stories. They see stories as a way of understanding our experiences, a means by which we form our identity, and a method for making sense out of larger social and cultural issues. They describe different kinds of narratives—cultural narratives, family narratives, individual narratives, and organizational narratives. They are not writing specifically about narrative learning in conjunction with transformative learning, but it is easy to take the small step from one to the other. If people tell and read stories to make sense out of their experiences, understand their identity, and understand social and cultural issues, this is all a part of how transformative learning takes place. Tennant

(2012), for example, introduces the concept of the "storied self" in his discussion of understanding the potential for transformation.

Jarvis (2012) suggests several ways that fiction and film can have the potential to engage people in transformative experiences: they can connect with others who live very different lives from their own; they can have intense emotional responses and fears; they can stand back and see the world from a distance; they can identify the discourses that shape their lives; they can be led to ideology critique; and they can actively construct their role as a reader.

In keeping with our storytelling theme, Patricia tells a story about her engagement with reading a story (Cranton, 2012).

Patricia: I am an indiscriminate reader of fiction. I become as engaged with a thriller in which corpses show up on every other page in various states of disrepair as I do with John Updike and Margaret Atwood and Alice Munro (our celebrated Canadian recipient of the Nobel Prize of Literature), Jane Austen and Thomas Mann. As I was contemplating how reading fiction has the potential to foster critical reflection, critical self-reflection, and perhaps transformative learning, I happened to read a novel that disturbed me deeply. It was a simple enough story, really. A young woman was homeless and struggling to remain a university student. She camped out in a cold, deserted, abandoned farm house with her dog. She and her dog kept each other warm at night, shared food, and gave each other love and companionship. There was a dream-like quality to the novel, the writing was lyrical, and symbolic animals and birds populated the pages. But then, the young woman fell in love with one of her professors, a man considerably older than she was. As she spent more and more time with the man, I read faster and faster, worried sick about the dog. I skimmed over the development of the human relationship, the revealing of dark secrets between woman and man, not giving a fig what they were up to. What about the dog? The woman went out to see the dog less and less frequently. The dog grew thin, matted, and sad. In a scene I could barely look at long enough to read, the woman killed her dog.

Initially, I did not understand why I reacted so strongly to this particular story. I did not understand it, in fact, until I realized the meaning of Clark and Rossiter's (2008) suggestion that we position ourselves in the stories we read. I have lived with dogs for my whole life. During this time, there have been many different dogs, and some tragedies. Positioning myself in this story brought to consciousness a great fear that I have neglected or could neglect my dogs in such a way so as to put their lives in danger. This was an important (and difficult) insight for me, and one that I could relate to reoccurring dreams, and fears that I experience in relationships in general.

The chapter establishes the groundwork for the stories that follow in Chapters 4 through 8 and, we hope, gives a strong rationale for how we, as practitioners can make foster transformative learning so as to make a difference for individuals, organizations, and society.

SUMMARY

This chapter is intended to provide an introduction to the book as a whole. We opened the chapter with a brief discussion of how making a difference is a goal of adult educators. We included an overview of transformative learning theory as it currently exists in the literature. We then made a case for developing and acting upon a unified or integrated theory of transformative learning. We included a section on narrative learning and learning through reading fiction and writing creative non-fiction. In the spirit of storytelling we included brief stories of our own experiences with transformative learning and stories. In the next chapters, we turn toward a more detailed discussion of storytelling and transformative learning, and then turn to the first-person stories we solicited from adult educators and learners.

UNDERSTANDING SELF AND SOCIETY THROUGH STORYTELLING

One of the best gifts you have to offer when you write personal history is the gift of yourself. Give yourself permission to write about yourself, and have a good time doing it.

William Zinsser, *On Writing Well*, 2006, p. 146

"Did I tell you the story about the time a raccoon carried off my old cat?" "Could you tell me the story of how you became a teacher?" "There must be a story behind that!" "Remember the time our Aunt Gertie told us just what she thought of our garden?" So often, in conversations with friends, families, and students, we rely on stories to communicate important events in our lives, tell funny anecdotes to amuse listeners, or use a story to illustrate a point in a teaching and learning situation. When I [Patricia] encounter a lull in a discussion in an evening class when everyone is tired from a long work day and possibly suffering from missing supper as they drive straight from work to class, I tell a story. As soon as I say, "Would you like to hear a story about....?" students lean forward and smile and nod. The story may only take a few minutes, but the simple act of storytelling re-energizes, encourages laughter, and refocuses participants' attention on the group.

One time, I went overboard with my story. It was a fairly typical story about my dogs, one of whom killed a groundhog. I have lived with dogs all of my life, and I grew up on a farm, where the dogs were less civilized than "city dogs." I still prefer uncivilized dogs, dogs who are closer to nature, dogs who tend to reject wearing bows and bandanas and don't much like walking on leashes. They would rather run through the woods and be dogs rather than possessions. So, I embarked on a story of my dog killing a groundhog. I didn't scrimp on the details. I told how the dog got the groundhog by the back of the neck and shook him to death, which is what dogs do. I then went on to tell how my dog ate the groundhog, *the whole thing,* I said. I was prepared to go on with how my dog then threw up the groundhog, but I noticed a few of my students looking quite pale, so I caught myself, and ended the story before the ending. I explained, we laughed, and everyone was engaged for the rest of the evening.

In this chapter, we introduce the second framework for the book—storytelling. There are several approaches to storytelling in the literature ranging from Rossiter and Clark's (2007) concept of narrative learning, to Tyler and Swartz's (2012) and Boje's (2007) use of storytelling in organizations, and to Clark's (2012) understanding of "embodied narrative." We do not intend to engage in a detailed theoretical discussion here, but rather to introduce the readers to how we understand ourselves, our experiences, our identities, and the world we live in through stories.

NARRATIVE LEARNING

Narrative learning and narrative knowledge are commonly referred to in the adult education literature, as is narrative inquiry, a research methodology using stories that has become popular in recent years. Rossiter and Clark (2007) provide an excellent overview of narrative learning and narrative knowing with a focus on the practicalities of facilitating narrative learning in the classroom. They open their book with individual stories from both authors, an introduction which gives an idea of how narrative learning can facilitate learning. The authors describe narrative as a "basic structure through which we make meaning of our lives" (p. 13). They remind us that human life is more than a "list of happenings," but rather it is a process of understanding what those happenings mean within the context of our lives and within the context of the larger picture—the society within which we live. Clark and Rossiter emphasize the importance of stories in our individual lives and also in our cultural and social experiences, an emphasis which fits well with our goals in this book. As they say, "our lives are steeped in stories" (p.20)—cultural narratives, individual narratives, family narratives, and organizational narratives. The concept of a "storied life" suggests that the nature of individuals' identity is an "unfolding story" (p. 44).

Clark and Rossiter (2008) describe the essential features of narrative learning: hearing stories, telling stories, and recognizing stories. They see stories as a way of understanding our experiences, a means by which we form our identity, and a method for making sense out of larger social and cultural issues. The hearing of stories draws us into an experience "at more than a cognitive level" (p. 65). They engage learners at a deeper and more holistic level (though the groundhog story might be an exception). In the telling of stories, the learner is at the center of the narrative; he or she tells of experiences and links those experiences with the content of the discussion. In recognizing stories, learners see how they are positioned in narratives, including narratives that are related to their culture, society, race, gender, and background.

Learning from fiction is a somewhat different spin on narrative learning, but it is closely related and worth mentioning here. Jarvis (2006) says that fiction can offer disorienting dilemmas, encourage dialogue where contradictions can emerge, lead to imagining alternatives, and allow for the trying on of different points of view. Jarvis derives her ideas from research she conducted in a college classroom using popular romantic fiction. Her participants were women from different ethnic and social backgrounds and women of different ages who were preparing for entry into higher education. Jarvis (2012) suggests several ways that fiction and film can have the potential to engage people in transformative experiences: they can connect with others who live very different lives from their own; they can have intense emotional responses and fears; they can stand back and see the world from a distance; they can identify the discourses that shape their lives; they can be led to ideology critique; and they can actively construct their role as a reader. We discuss the ways in which transformative learning can occur through reading and telling stories more fully in Chapter 3.

STORYTELLING

There are differences among scholars who write about storytelling, but aside from some debate about terminology, most seem to be talking about the same thing. We find Nelson's (2009) discussion of the purpose of stories in learning to be a good place to start. She lists the following purposes of telling and listening to stories:

- Respect for all of life, including respect for self, family, community, tribe, and planet.
- The interconnectedness of all life.
- The coherence in one's life from the past and the hope in one's life for the future.
- The awareness that adversity will come in life.
- The goals of building a life in harmony and balance with nature.
- The ability to laugh at pitfalls.
- How to stay safe.
- Identification with a group or tribe.
- Character traits such as courage, perseverance, ability, and bravery.
- Role modeling by characters withstanding negative forces and overcoming adversity.
- Acceptance of one's role or destiny in life (p. 210).

In other words, stories are used to address most of the things we think about (or could think about) in our daily lives. Many of us may not think about "respect for all of life" on a regular basis, but it is there, somewhere in the back of our minds, as is the interconnectedness of all life. Stories bring these issues to the fore of our consciousness.

Nelson points out that many stories use the hero/heroine journey as an outline for a plot. She suggests that understanding the stages in a story show how listeners and readers gain a sense of emotional resiliency through being involved in storytelling and story listening. The hero's stages as documented by Campbell (1972) include:

- *Normal.* Life is in a steady state, but then a "call to adventure" changes everything.
- *Separation.* The character leaves home to prove his or her character or to help others.
- *Tests.* The character goes through a variety of serious tests (for example, battles, journeys into the unknown).
- *Return.* The hero or heroine returns and brings back the knowledge to the community (p. 211).

In Canada, on Sunday at noon, people from across the country tune into *The Vinyl Café* to listen to Stuart McLean tell stories. He has been doing this for decades, and most Canadians are familiar with the lives of Dave and Morley and their son Sam, and a whole host of supporting characters who live in the neighborhood. The stories are often funny, but not always, and they always contain a central gem, a meaning that all listeners can connect with—conflicts between neighbors, love between spouses, the trials of raising and caring for a child. Perhaps best of all, the stories are told to live audiences in different cities and towns, so people can go and listen in person; but those listening to the radio are quite aware the audience is present as Stuart McLean hesitates to wait for an audience reaction, or unexpectedly laughs at his own story. The purposes of storytelling that Nelson (2009) lists are evident in Stuart McLean's stories as are the stages or elements in a story. The "adventure" may be Dave trying to get up on the roof of his neighbors' house with a magnet to erase a rude message he inadvertently left on their answering machine; the separation may be Sam running away from home; and the test may be figuring out how to work through difficult family problems. People living ordinary lives are living heroes' lives.

The Storied Life

People use stories to shape their identities. We are the stories we tell. In his workshops and conference presentations, Bill Randall, who writes about how we story and restory our lives (for example, see Kenyon & Randall, 1977), often tells his "iron lung" story. He remembers being in an iron lung as a child, which was, at the time, a response to polio. For years, he told this story to colleagues, to students, and to friends at parties. On one occasion, he was telling the story to an audience which included a family member. The family member was shocked. "What? An iron lung? You were never in an iron lung!" But Bill was convinced he had been. The family member proved to be right, and Bill came to understand how individuals restory their lives as they search for meaningful ways of understanding themselves. We said earlier, in Chapter 1, that transformative learning is based on constuctivism—the notion that individuals construct meaning from their experiences in different ways and that different people see the same event in their own ways. Storytelling shares this foundation. Two siblings, for example, may have quite different memories of shared childhood events. Two people in a long-term relationship may have different perceptions of how they met or how they felt about each other when they met.

Tennant (2012) says that autobiographical stories are usually related to a particular problem or issue, and they lead to "concerns about the self, such as self-esteem, self-satisfaction, well-being, self-doubt, and self-efficacy" (p. 89). But then comes the interesting issue. An educator (or any listener) can accept that the story is true for the person who told it and respond accordingly. Or the educator can challenge the story in order to encourage the storyteller to explore alternative interpretations. Going back to Patricia's story in Chapter 1, the listener could say, "I understand how deeply you were affected by what was happening to the dog in the story; this must have been so difficult for you." At this point, the educator or listener supports the storyteller and that is really the end of that. But if the educator asks, "What did the dog mean to you? Why was this fictional dog so important to you? What did the dog represent in your life? Have you ever experienced or thought about killing your own dog?" Then the storyteller is provoked into seeing her story differently. She may react with anger or distress and close down the conversation, but it also may be the case that she continues to think about the questions.

A few years ago I (Patricia) had a storytelling experience that stays fresh in my mind. I was attending a meeting of adult educators at Teachers College in New York City. The purpose of the meeting has faded from my memory, but the storytelling exercise has not. Jo Tyler led an activity on storytelling. We worked with a partner, and my partner was my colleague, Victoria Marsick, from Teachers College. Jo asked us to think back to a significant event in our practice as adult educators; she gave us time to reflect on this on our own. We were then asked to tell the story of the experience to our partner. The partner was asked to listen without interruption. Next, our partner told the story back to us. Inevitably, the story sounded different. Jo asked us to re-tell our story. This time, our partner could comment and ask questions. Finally, Jo asked us to tell the same story from the perspective of the main character in the story. I had told a story that I have written about before—the story of Jim, a tradesperson who was taking a course in adult education in preparation for teaching his trade. Jim was older than other learners in the course, and he was desperately frightened of being in a university course. He coped with this by being the "funny guy" in the group. But Jim broke down in about the second week of a six-week intensive residential course. He said, "I can't do it! I can't be a teacher! What am I doing?" I quickly broke up the class. Jim was not especially comfortable with me, a female instructor. The class included mostly men, so I asked some of the guys to take Jim for a walk in the woods or to the pub, or whatever they thought best.

When I told my story from Jim's perspective, an astonishing thing happened. I truly felt like I was Jim speaking. I even adopted his strong Canadian Maritime accent and his language choices. This was not a conscious decision, and I hardly realized it until my partner Victoria pointed it out to me. I had put myself into Jim's reality, and I spoke his story. I had reflected on Jim's story extensively, but this experience of telling the story, having a good listener, retelling the story, and telling the story from Jim's perspective gave me insights I had not had before. I can't say that I fully understood Jim's perspective, but I came much closer to understanding it when I spoke the story in his voice. I was able to position myself in his story by making a connection between his experience and the experiences of my brothers, my son, and my father, all of whom were tradespeople. I think this illustrates the centrality of the storied life. My storied life was, on the surface, very different from Jim's storied life. But when it came down to it, I could see the way that our stories overlapped and gain a much better understanding of his experience than I ever could have had without the stories.

Identity is that sense of a core self that essentially remains the same over time even though there are multiple facets to individuals' lives that change and are constructed in response to life events. Identity is expressed in a person's authenticity (being real and genuine in the expression of oneself) and becoming authentic is also a transformative learning process (Cranton & Carusetta, 2004). In this way, the strands all come together. Storytelling defines a person's identity and sense of self. There is a core self that is relatively constant over time. Yet, that self or aspects of that self may be challenged by other events and experience. In this case, the person may choose to question her assumptions and beliefs, and may challenge her story or her restory. If this happens, transformative learning is a possibility.

Jo Tyler, the excellent facilitator of the activity Patricia described above, has worked with storytelling in organizations and has written about this extensively. We turn to this application of storytelling next.

Storytelling in Organizations

Tyler and Swartz (2012) follow the work of Boje (2001) in distinguishing between "stories" and "narratives." As they define it, storytelling is the oral telling of a personal experience. It is not mediated by technology and it does not get told in print. It is not a performance, but rather it is a relational and emergent exchange that "depends on both listening and poststory conversation" (p. 455). Storytelling is a natural form of human communication, and we can all recall telling and listening to stories. Stories turn into narratives when they are told and retold. During that process, they become practiced and edited. Bill Randall's "iron lung story" would be considered a narrative under this definition, as would Patricia's story of Jim. A narrative ends up with a crafted plot—a beginning, middle, and end.

Stories are dynamic rather than static, organic rather than mechanistic, and emergent rather than linear according to Tyler and Swartz (2012, p. 459). What we find particularly interesting about Tyler and Swartz's perspective on stories is that stories are alive—they are changing (as Bill Randall's concept of restorying addresses), they possess a sort of life force, and they are inspired in the telling. At first, this sounds just a bit silly. Stories are alive? What might that mean? Boje and Tyler (2009) explain that stories have many authors, stories have a collective force, and stories have shifting meanings. If we think about this using ordinary language, it means that we tell stories differently depending on who is the listener. The listener has the potential of shaping the story, and the meaning shifts. This is demonstrated well in Patricia's experience of telling her story to a partner, hearing the story told back to her, and telling the story again with the listener's perspective in mind. If I (Patricia) tell a story to my brother, with whom I share decades of memories and experiences, it will be quite a different story from one that I might tell a colleague or a student, even though the topic of the story might be the same.

Boje (2006) is interested in how all of this plays out in organizational learning through storytelling. He maintains the distinction between narrative and story as mentioned previously. Narratives have a "proper" linear plot, something that Boje believes is rare in storytelling in organizations. He proposes that "one is well advised to also be studying the more "improper," less linear stories, and more to the point, study *systemicity* of story-dialogicality behaviors of people in organizations, in relationship to more petrified narrative-coherence "behaviors (p. 3)"

Boje writes:

While teaching at UCLA's management school (1978-1986), I began sneaking off with the Folklore and Mythology faculty and doctoral students; they were tucked away behind the library of the Anderson School of Management. Professors Georges and Jones, for example, were pioneering a new approach called "organization folklore," a rebellion against traditional obsession with collecting fairytales, Native American coyote tales, and working-folk-stories, and then meticulously classifying them with motif-index, or showing how my themes migrated with population from old world to new.

Something was being missed. Organization folklorists weren't looking at the *behavior of people* telling stories in organizations. That sounds simple enough, and I am not saying it was never done, only that the narrow definitions of story-must-be-narrative plot put blinders on researchers being able to see systemicity complexity of story behaviors. (p. 5)

Boje (2006) went on to describe the "storytelling organization" (p. 8) using case studies of several organizations, including Disney World, Nike, and Enron. He defines a storytelling organization as "a collective system[icity] in which the performance of stories is a key part of members' sensemaking and a means to allow them to supplement individual memories with institutional memory" (p. 7).

The practical side of telling stories in organizations receives less attention in this literature than does the theoretical side. But when we think of how Jo Tyler brought out our stories in the session described earlier, it is easy to imagine how this activity and similar activities could work within an organization to bring people together and understand each other's perspectives in a way that could not be accomplished without stories.

Embodied Narrative

"The body has many stories," writes Clark (2012, p. 426). Embodied learning emphasizes that knowing is not only a cognitive process; we "know in and through our bodies" (p. 426). Some scholars suggest that learning begins and occurs in our bodies, not in the cognitive reflection on our experiences. It is through narrative knowing that we make sense of this experience by storying it. What does this mean? If we ask ourselves where we feel fear or anxiety or joy in our body, most people can easily respond to this question. I feel fear in my lower back, for example; another person may feel fear in his arms or legs. I feel joy in my blood, coursing through my body; another person may feel joy in his heart.

Clark (2012) tells a story about physical decline associated with aging: her experience with osteoarthritis. In Chapter 5, we see a similar story by Laurence Robert Cohen, not associated with aging, but with illness. Clark had her knee replaced with a mechanical device. She personalized this new knee by naming her "Daisy," and she writes about life before and after Daisy, describing this as a transformative learning experience. In her chapter, Clark provides a series of vignettes: rewinding the tape (where she looks for but cannot find the beginning of her story), claiming agency by giving in (where she realized she needed surgery), becoming an object to be fixed (the events leading up to the surgery), and being overtaken (being a body to be acted on). Then her story shifts from "I can't" to "I can," which she describes as "more than a little wonderful" (p. 434). But at the same time, she recognizes that she is disabled and enmeshed in the narrative of a physical disability.

This story introduces a facet of storytelling we have not yet recognized in this chapter. Clark concludes:

> So welcoming Daisy has meant that I'm in a new narrative now, a narrative that is embodied in a way that I didn't know was possible when my body was well and able, qualities that kept my body distant, and often separate, from my understanding of myself. That distance is gone now. I don't *have* a body as I once did—I *am* my body.

This understanding of storytelling underlines the holistic nature of stories and narratives. A story is not a simple cognitive recollection of a series of events. It involves emotions, imagination, and our bodies. For this book we are less concerned about whether stories are called stories or narratives and are more concerned about how they can demonstrate the ways people change. In this way, as we explore in Chapter 3 and also in Chapter 10, storytelling supports an integrated theory of transformative learning.

My Day In Italy

This is a story of a typical day during my (Michael) three month stay in Italy. An earlier version was published in the University of Idaho's College of Education *Envision* magazine.

> I wake early and the story of my day begins. I want to go over my lessons for the day and sometimes that takes some time. My second floor apartment is roomy – a living room, two bedrooms, kitchen, bathroom, and laundry room. The laundry room is my favorite because there is a table where I work and eat, and an open window with a rack outside where I hang my laundry to dry. I had not used clothespins for many years but the apartment has no dryer. Dropping a sock or pillowcase is not unusual. The very small washing machine takes a

couple of hours per load. I laugh to myself, imagining someone from the street below spotting the brand and current status of my underwear, shirts, and other garments.

Out the expansive, open window sits the FIAT headquarters and sometimes I see a helicopter landing atop. More pleasing to me is the ebb and flow of people walking by, perhaps on a Sunday stroll, perhaps headed to the Lingotto mall sitting next to the FIAT building, or perhaps hurrying to the metro or bus stop just a block and a half away. It engages my romantic spirit to be in the midst of Italian humanity and to imagine the lives of those who live here. I linger at my window often.

The lessons I review are sometimes for classes I am teaching. Other times they are for the Italian courses I am taking. At age 61, learning a new language is hard but so very rewarding. It is, just a little, transformative for me to take on the Italian persona through the language. I feel more "in the role" of an Italian wannabe, just as I have felt when an actor in plays years-past, and I find myself "speaking" with my whole body – hands and arms and even eye brows.

I attempt to speak Italian everywhere I go and the Italians are unvaryingly helpful and appreciative that I am giving it a go. Once, endeavoring to find lodging for the night in Venice, I walked into a hotel I knew was totally booked and the manager not only found a room for me but dropped the room rate by 20 Euros just because I was talking with him in Italian. Or trying my best to do so. On the way to my room I chortled to myself, prouder than I should have been for someone who knew almost nothing. My hard work studying prepositions, verbs in their many forms, phrases; looking up word after word after word after word; asking for help constantly – had paid off. I realize I can take care of myself.

Leaving my apartment each morning I walk across the street to a "bar" where I order a cappuccino, brioche, and a sprumata, which is fresh-squeezed orange juice. Luciana and Geno, the proprietors, know me well, greet me warmly, and help me with an Italian word here and there or share travel directions to places I am planning to visit. They were excited when my wife Lana arrived for five weeks – they fell in love with her and vice versa – and sad when she left for home.

On the days I teach or take classes, I then make the five minute walk to school. I arrive just in time for my Italian class, enjoying the luxury of being a student. Class lasts two hours and then, 15 minutes later, I teach for three hours. The long stretch is tiring but rewarding.

On the way home (I think of it as home) I stop by a small restaurant for lunch. The simple plate of spaghetti is inexpensive and scrumptious. Unlike most of my hurried meals in the United States I take all the time I want. Feeling the luxury of experiencing the moment fully. Reading – trying to read – a newspaper, perhaps *La Stampa*. Listening to the conversations surrounding me. Reflecting. Basking in just-being. After, if I need to buy food, down the street is the neighborhood grocery store. If I forget and my timing is not right I am out of luck, the shop closed for an extended lunchtime period well into the afternoon. Again, I laugh at myself and my habits of 61 years.

If I have a free afternoon I hop on the metro or bus and head to downtown Torino or other nearby locales. I do not drive a car for the three months I spend in Italy. I do walk. A lot. An Italian once told me that despite the delicious food many visitors lose weight during their time in Italy because they walk so much. This was not my experience.

Torino is filled with history, museums, palaces, and awe inspiring churches and I am enthralled with the richness of experience I receive during my stay. My last evening in Italy I went to downtown Torino to say goodbye in my heart. Walking there, I decided that I would visit every church I passed along my way. Each touched my soul and I can't explain why. Perhaps it was the beautiful artistry. Perhaps it was knowing that I was interconnecting with centuries of worshipers who too had sought solace and inspiration and hope. Perhaps it was the sadness of leaving combined with the anticipation of heading home, symbolized by Christ on the cross, that made each church meaningful.

On days I don't have classes I might catch a train and take a day trip to a town not far away. Those trips, to places like La Sacra di San Michele (St. Michael's Abbey) are sometimes as meaningful to me as more extended visits to Rome, Florence, Venice, Milan, or Cinque Terra.

I am not a food aficionado, so dinner is simple. My favorite, a margherita pizza, is said to have been named after Queen Margherita over a century ago. It has three colors – red (tomato), green (basil), and white (mozzarella) - representing the Italian flag. Occasionally I get an urge for home and on the way to my apartment I drop by the cinema not to see a film but to pick up some movie popcorn and a diet soda.

My last stop is the neighborhood gelateria where I buy a gelato, which is Italian ice cream. Many do the same, strolling down the street with cone in hand, which I find a very civilized practice. The store is run by Gio and Giovanna. Gio always makes friendly fun of me when I try to order in Italian but after a certain number of times I remember the correct word, gender, and number and we have a nice laugh. It seems that everyone in Italy is my language teacher. As everyone's student, I am a humble learner and grateful to each person who takes a little extra of their time to help me. It is interesting, but the simple act of trying to speak in Italian, with the laughs and missteps and the help of others, connects me with people in ways I would never have been able to otherwise.

Walking up the stairs to my apartment I unlock the heavily bolted door. I have a television but I don't watch it. Why waste the time? Instead I transfer pictures I've taken during the day to my computer. I drink un bicchiere di vino rosso o una birra italiana. I try to read an Italian novel I bought, tediously translating most words. I check my iPad to see what is happening around the world and especially in the United States. Since Torino is eight hours earlier than Boise this is a good time to Skype or to carry on an electronic conversation with folks from home.

I am on my own most of my stay. Lana is there for five wonderful weeks, arriving with two of our close friends who visit for a week and then leave for Rome. We see much together until she leaves for Boise and then I am by myself again. But I rarely, rarely feel alone. I begin to feel – just a little – like I am part of the neighborhood. Even though we all know I am a passing stranger, I get to know a bit about what it means to live less as a tourist than most and more like a piece of the interconnected community. People I see often know a little of my life and I know a little of theirs. This great country has opened up its arms to me and I have seen a fleck of it, enough to enthrall me.

Regardless of weather, I open my windows wide and watch the Italian night. I try to remember how to conjugate the word *fare* and review the tricky Italian prepositions. Buses rumble by. I climb into bed and close my eyes, content.

SUMMARY

In this chapter, we provided an overview of the second theoretical framework for this book—storytelling. We paid attention to the work of Rossiter and Clark who have been leaders in bringing the attention of adult educators to narrative learning and narrative knowledge in their books and articles. Clark and Rossiter describe the essential features of narrative learning: hearing stories, telling stories, and recognizing stories, all of which play a significant role in how storytelling contributes to and fosters transformative learning. We included Tyler and Swartz's work and Boje's theoretical development related to storytelling in organizations. What is especially interesting about their approach is the way they distinguish between "narratives" and "stories." And finally, we have addressed the recent trend to incorporate embodied learning in our understanding of adult learning. Carolyn Clark's (2012) chapter in *The Handbook of Transformative Learning* is an excellent illustration of the connection between these two constructs. We have included stories—our own and the stories of others—throughout the chapter to illustrate the power of storytelling.

TRANSFORMATIVE LEARNING THROUGH STORYTELLING

Midway in our life's journey, I went astray from the straight road and woke to find myself alone in a dark wood.

The Divine Comedy, Dante Alighieri, Dante & Ciardi, 2003, p. 16

It seems that to find the real path we have to go *off* the path we are now on, even for an instant, and earn the privilege of losing our way. As the path fades, we are forced to take a good look at the life in which we actually find ourselves.

The Heart Aroused, David Whyte, 1994, p. 25

There is a remarkable parallel between transformative learning and storytelling. Transformative learning is about making meaning of experiences and revising perspectives when experiences are encountered that are discrepant with previous assumptions and beliefs. Storytelling is a way of making meaning of experiences in all cultures and across all times. There are stories remaining in our culture that were first told before they could be recorded with the written word. If we turn our minds to fiction, poetry, music, and art in general, we find stories told in a variety of formats over the centuries. It is our goal here to bring these two strands together—transformative learning and storytelling—in order to enhance both the theory and practice of transformative education.

Stories of the assassination of U.S. President John Kennedy and of his pledge to send a man to the moon and back by the end of the 1960's have been shared in classrooms, international media, and interpersonally for decades. One is a tragedy that at the time was a shocking transformational learning moment for people around the world; the other was an inspiring example of visionary leadership that transformed what people believed could be possible. Canadian astronaut Chris Hadfield used social media to communicate with students in classrooms, news media, and ordinary citizens during his remarkable six-month time in space. He created an unforgettable story of not only space travel, but of how to communicate with the world while he was in space. The actual events and the stories about those events have impacted millions of people. They are a part of our global lore. But we can also go back in time to understand the power of stories. For example, stories about World War I and World War II still appeal to readers who want to understand the historical context of their social world. Even further back in time, stories about the Roman Empire and the history of China entrance readers today. Stories have power, and we use stories to make sense of our personal experiences as well as the events that change the world we live in.

STORIES LEADING TO TRANSFORMATION

Stories result in transformative learning if they lead individuals to experience a disorienting dilemma—a disjuncture (Jarvis, 2008) between their current beliefs and those the story evokes, and then a subsequent change to their perspectives including their views of themselves and the world. Almost everyone who lives in North America and perhaps beyond, can tell the story of where he or she was during 9/11/01. Stories of the Kennedy assassination and the challenge to go to the moon and back have long been a part of the experience of the citizens of the world. Kennedy has been written about and discussed so often that anyone reading these stories again or in more detail would be unlikely to experience a disorienting dilemma since the stories are now so familiar that they are a part of our understanding of history. Like Kennedy's call to go to the moon and back nearly four decades earlier, Chris Hadfield's openly and widely shared experiences recently led millions of people to realize that "anything is possible." Children across Canada were speaking on the radio to announce that they wanted to become scientists, astronauts, or engineers. Stories that change the world of possibilities have the potential to be transformative.

The United States' version of *The Vinyl Café* (see Chapter 2) is probably Garrison Keillor's *Prairie Home Companion,* a weekly radio performance that is conducted in front of a live audience. Similar to Stuart McLean, Keillor tells stories every week about a mythical town called Lake Wobegon, Minnesota, which has its own set of unique characters. The stories are humorous and told in the spirit of anecdotes. In spite of the anecdotal and humorous nature of the stories, they are about people living everyday lives and their experiences. In this way, they have the potential to lead listeners to a reconsideration of their memories and stories from their own lives. This, in turn, can foster transformative learning, as all good stories do.

We experience disorienting dilemmas that result in revised perspectives of our own lives or events in the world. Dirkx (2000) points out that most often transformative learning is a product of everyday experience rather than a "burning bush" phenomenon. This is what we see in the storytelling of Stuart McLean and Garrison Keillor. On a personal level, changes can be "small" paradigm shifts (Barker, 1985; Kuhn, 1962), or as Mezirow says, revisions to meaning schemes rather than to meaning perspectives. And, now and then, people experience profound shifts in their understanding of their lives. Mezirow's (1991) distinction between the revision of meaning schemes (beliefs, values, and assumptions) and the revision of meaning perspectives (world views, webs of assumptions and beliefs) is a useful way of understanding the levels or depths of transformative learning. On a larger scale, there can be a shift in the assumptions or perspectives of many members of an entire community, country, or world. The bombing of the twin towers in the United States on 9/11/01 caused a profound and immediate shift in the assumptions about the security of the United States not only by US citizens but by members of the world community. This was what Mezirow (2000) calls an epochal transformation. It was traumatic and caused major shifts not only in public policy but also in personal lives. The event led to a revision of assumptions and perspectives related to a wide range of issues that continue to impact the world today. The stories of this event are told time and again for a variety of purposes.

In another example, the incremental shifts in the perspectives in the United States and Canada regarding same-sex marriage or the legalization of marijuana are taking place over time but are no less profound. These shifts too have been built on stories. People who may not have had these experiences directly hear of them in the news, read about them in the paper, or learn about them from other sources, such as friends or family, and their assumptions are revised and revised again until public opinion is so strongly transformed that governmental policies and personal practices profoundly change.

INDIVIDUALS MAKING MEANING THROUGH STORIES

What is profound and what is deep depends on the individual who is engaged in the transformative experience. What may be a minor shift for one person can be a deeply insightful experience for another individual. Once a perspective has changed it cannot be undone. Once a person "knows," it is impossible to go back to not knowing. Still, when we talk about transformative learning we focus on significant, impactful changes to the assumptions that are the foundation of a personal worldview. How much difference a perspective change makes will range from the superficial to the deep, reoriented, maturing individuation that scholars such as Dirkx feel is important for transformative learning. We may be conscious of these underlying assumptions we hold, or we may not even know we hold them until something, such as a story or an experience, makes them problematic and therefore something we need to explore.

A central concept in transformative learning theory is that individuals make meaning of their experiences and revise that meaning based on new experiences that are discrepant with their previous points of view. Similarly, a central concept in the storytelling literature is that we make sense of our lives through stories. It is this intersection between transformative learning and storytelling that interests us in this chapter and in this book as a whole. Sometimes stories simply reinforce currently held beliefs. It is easy enough in the internet-driven world to seek out only those stories that support our current beliefs, and in this case, stories do not lead to transformative learning. But when people tell stories or position themselves in stories told by others, the stories can create disorienting dilemmas and then they have the potential to become transformative. Of course, the stories can be valuable regardless of their transformative potential, as they entertain, reinforce existing values or beliefs, instruct, motivate, or provide vicarious learning (Bandura, 1997).

Readers are able to see how others have negotiated specific events, and therefore may find the stories in this book to be transformative, instructive, or both.

Looking at this from another perspective, stories about major events may be significantly transformative but not result in transformative learning as it has been defined. For example, the 9/11/01 bombing of the twin towers in New York City was devastating and surely transformative for many. Deeply held assumptions about national and personal security were revised. The psyche of the citizens of the world changed. Billions have been spent as a nation revised its security systems and developed and staffed "Homeland Security." Even more importantly, this event led people around the world to view others from different countries in a new way. But we can ask whether this transformative was learning according to the definition offered in Chapter 1. Did people's assumptions become more open, more permeable, more discriminating, and more justified? Maybe not. It could be that people's assumptions were closed down, made narrower. All of a sudden, it was important to be suspicious of people from a different culture or with a different skin color. What is important about this example is that revisions of individuals' perspectives are not necessarily more open, permeable, and discriminating.

Some people will have been affected in ways that reflect a more open and better justified view of the world. Some will have revised assumptions to make them more narrow, prejudiced, and biased—this is not transformative learning, but rather a change that is inherently negative. Transformative learning is mostly an individual process, and individuals react to stories and events in ways that are unique to them.

STORIES THAT FACILITATE TRANSFORMATIVE LEARNING

Storytelling is a way to share examples of transformative learning and also a way to facilitate transformative learning. These goals may work together or separately. The story of how any religious leader going through some kind of conversion experience was transformed may or may not be used to create a transformative learning situation for followers or potential followers. It might be also used to reinforce current doctrine or ideology. Nelson Mandela's (1994) autobiography, *Long Walk to Freedom,* might not be a story of Mandela's transformation as much as an opportunity for readers to experience an "aha" moment about how to create a successful life. All stories can be transformative for some individuals but not for others.

Stories can be told in a wide variety of mediums—novels, plays, movies, television, biography, campfire stories, bedtime stories, music, and poetry—and in every genre, such as comedy, tragedy, thriller, romance, horror, documentary, fiction, and non-fiction. The famous six-word short-short story, "For sale: baby shoes, never worn," attributed to Ernest Hemingway (unsubstantiated), suggests a disorienting dilemma that has occurred for a young couple and their family. It is left up to the readers to fill in the missing parts of the story, and in doing so they may well call on their life experiences. *The Mists of Avalon* (Bradley, 1982), all 876 pages of it, tells the Arthurian legend from the perspective of the female characters. Reading it was a transformational experience for me (Michael) because, as one who had loved watching the musical Camelot and reading about that legend, I realized—I should say I was awakened in the sense of an "aha" experience as I read it—that the same events could result in two very different stories, interpretations, and accompanying perspectives, and that my simplistic idealism and romanticism could hardly explain the complexity of the situation or, indeed, of any situation.

Some books have instigated the transformation of so many individual world views that one might say that societal perspectives have been transformed. It can happen with a book of fiction—for example, Orwell's 1984 (1949) or Sinclair's The Jungle (1906)—or non-fiction, such as Carson's Silent Spring (1964). Sometimes these books have been stories, sometimes not, but books, like every other form of communication, have the power to radically transform belief systems when individuals are presented with a disorienting dilemma. Edward T. Hall's book, The Silent Language (1973), which I (Michael) read while taking a non-verbal communication class decades ago, was a transformative learning experience. It opened up an entire world that I had never even imagined and changed the way I have thought about communication ever since.

When I (Patricia) contemplated what stories were transformative learning experiences in my own life, I felt stymied. It seems that every book I have read (with some minor exceptions) has opened up new perspectives for me, and I hesitate about which ones I would describe as transformative, but I feel changed by all that I read. I am currently re-reading Shirley Jackson's (2005) short stories, including her well-known The Lottery, a story that stunned me when I first read it and one that continues to haunt me. In this story, there is a social norm or practice—the lottery—in which citizens of a community choose a number or a ticket and the person who is chosen is stoned to death. This is a metaphor, of course, for the way we treat people in our culture and communities, but it is a fairly transparent metaphor, and a devastating one. It reminds me of the residential schools in Canada; it reminds me of the fishers and farmers in Nova Scotia in the early 1900s. Stephen King's (2009) Under the Dome, falls into the horror genre, which one does not usually associate with profound insights and transformative events, but when read as a (very long, nearly 1100 pages) metaphor, it takes on a different light. I read this book when it first came out, in 2009, and it seems there is hardly a week that goes by when I do not think about the story. In a deceptively simple story line, a huge impenetrable dome descends over an area, cutting off those under the dome from the rest of the world. Environmental issues, sources of food, social issues, aggression, competition, and finally desperation set in, and the reader watches humanity degenerate.

I digress. I give these examples to illustrate that it is not only novels receiving critical acclaim that are meaningful in terms of their potential to engage readers in transformative learning. The story I intended to write about was by a recently discovered (by me) Canadian author, Bill Gaston, who has written marvelous, complex, and tragic psychological stories. The Cameraman (1994) is a story about Francis, who lives his life in the shadow of Koz. Francis is the cameraman. Koz is

29

the director. But Koz is elusive and has a deep shadow side. Koz is not his real name. Koz tells lies and more lies, and Francis cannot understand his life. Yet, Francis is under the spell of Koz. When Koz moves into filming his killing of his woman friend, and asks Francis to be yet again the cameraman, Francis finally tries to stop him and then to walk away when he cannot stop him.

This story stopped me in my tracks. I had taken it out of the library. I read it. I read it again. I bought the book so I could read it yet again and write in the margins. Without being aware of it during the initial readings, I saw myself in the story. I thought about how I have been drawn into others' views of the world. I remembered the occasions where I have been told that I was gullible. I remembered my mother's friend laughing at me when she told me that I had won the prize for the best apron in a community event, and I believed her. The novel called the concept of "reality" into question along with the question of consciousness. How do we know what is real? Are we looking through a camera lens or are we seeing reality? Is there a reality to be seen, or is what we see always socially constructed? I tried to hate Koz, for he was a liar, and I had an assumption that liars are despicable. But I couldn't hate Koz, so what did that mean about my assumptions related to truth and reality? I found Francis gullible and weak. But that did not work either. Francis was actually strong and loving. Through this kind of questioning, I became aware of aspects of myself that I had not acknowledged previously, and that increased self-awareness was transformative.

POSITIONING OURSELVES IN STORIES

We have all had experiences when stories transformed our belief systems dramatically. It is one thing to describe a situation in theoretical or statistical terms, it is quite another—much more personal, emotional, and immediate—to hear a story about the same situation. Either approach can be transformative, but the power of stories is to get quickly into our hearts and minds and to open us up to the possibility that we have been missing something in what we believe about the world or ourselves. In that sense music, often with the story in lyrics, can quickly move us as well. For example, the combination of music and story in musicals such as *Les Miserables* is especially powerful. It creates an account of personal struggle, victory, and defeat and carries messages about society and individuals that leads members of the audience to assess reified assumptions. Poetry has the same power, whether it is an epic poem such as Dante's *Divine Comedy*, or something more intimate, such as a poem from Pablo Neruda. The reader, perhaps, has to read more between the lines when discovering a poem but the story often resides within it just as much as it might in a biography or novel.

When a person reads or hears a striking story, the way that person thinks about the topic can be changed radically, as in Patricia's reading of *The Cameraman*. This could occur, for example, by listening to someone's testimony in church, hearing a story about how a person lost his life or how a life was saved, or it might come about from a best friend talking about a new lifestyle she tried which could not have been previously imagined and which utterly changed the way she thought about herself. Those stories can be transformative learning experiences. Although transformative learning through storytelling can occur serendipitously, it can also be instigated intentionally by mentors or teachers who present learners with situations. Koans for example, used in Zen Buddhism, force followers or learners to confront a problem that cannot be solved by logic (Watts, 1989).

Koans are "Mysterious stories used to teach Zen Buddhism for over a thousand years" (FitzPatrick, 2005, p. 957). Koans are seemingly unsolvable paradoxes used by Zen Masters with their students that cannot be solved by rational thinking. They can be in the form of stories, but also in phrases, sayings, anecdotes, or dialogues. These present conundrums that students cannot solve by using their existing assumptions, but only by looking at the situation completely differently. Contemplating koans can bring about a "state of enlightenment" (p. 958), or *satori*, which, using our frame of reference here, might also be considered disorienting dilemmas leading to transformative learning.

Franciscan priest Richard Rohr (2003) likens Jesus' parables to koans. By telling these stories Jesus, he says, tried to turn reality upside down, to "subvert the normal way of seeing" because "we are trapped, we can't see" (p. 34). Many of Jesus' images and parables, Rohr says, are "subversive" and about seeing. Four of the parables, for example, are about things that are lost or hidden, that followers have to want to see and to learn how to see.

Rohr is a mystic who writes about thinking that is not dualistic (Rohr, 2009). Jesus' first message in the Gospels, he says, which is usually translated as "convert" or "reform" or repent" is the Greek word *metanoia*, which means, to "change your mind." Great breakthrough moments he says are not changes in "what" people see but "how" (p. 62) they see. Conversion is not a one-time event, he says, and not something that is merely something that happens instantly as a one-time event. "True and full conversion (head, heart, gut)," he says, "does not really happen until the new program is in the hard-wiring and becomes a permanent and 'natural' trait rather than a one-time emotion. The process takes most of one's life, and is actually the very task of life and contemplation" (p. 62). He describes wisdom as not a gathering of more and more information but as a different way of seeing and knowing. The way he describes this process sounds very close to the phases Mezirow described as perspective transformation.

USING STORIES IN EDUCATION

Many educators use stories in their classes. As we discussed before, there are a number of ways stories can be used in a classroom to teach about topics as varied as ethics (Rabin & Smith, 2013), science (Horton, 2013), and art (Zander, 2007). Business schools use case studies—essentially a real story developed solely for instructional objectives—extensively. Someone in the business school might use

Alfred Sloan's (1994) autobiography, *My Years at General Motors*, to talk about strategy or organizational change. Someone teaching history might discuss Gandhi's walk to the sea or Martin Luther King's march on Washington. Nelson Mandela's story will be told in classrooms in a myriad of disciplines, to people of all ages, and for a variety of purposes. In colleges of education instructors tell stories of successes or failures, which bolster points they want to make about a lesson or to encourage thinking and dialogue. The media for these stories might be a film clip, a novel or short story, or simply a personal story from the teacher herself.

Educators do not have to go outside the classroom to find stories for learning. Many times, the stories come from the student's own lives (see Meyer, 2009, for example). The use of life histories for adult learners can be very powerful. The use of real, personal stories, rather than simply teaching the principles, concepts, and research around a topic, engages students at a much different level.

William Zinsser, who has authored many books about writing, says that regardless of the form – memoir, personal history, autobiography, family history—"writing about one's life is a powerful human need" (2004, p. 6). He was talking about the desire to leave a record behind for others, but writing personal stories, or life histories, can touch a human need, the need to make meaning out of one's life. Dominice (2000) advocates the use of educational biographies. Adult learners, using this method, develop life histories which they can use to reflect upon their educational experiences. This helps, he says, to give learners a deeper understanding of how they learn and about their existing knowledge. Using educational biographies for learning makes students "partners" in the process and engages them in collaborative inquiry. By looking at previous learning experiences learners can see when their own transformative learning has occurred. Looking at developmental transitions can create an increased readiness to learn and adults are empowered to take more responsibility for their learning. In this approach, adult learners are not receiving knowledge in the form of other's stories but are creating knowledge based on their own, personal life stories.

Jerold Apps' (1996) *Teaching from the Heart* is filled with personal stories and changed the way I (Michael) thought about teaching. Apps talks about his life-story writing workshops and how participants spend much of the time just sharing their stories with each other. The participants first write the stories, and then they share them in class. Insights come from remembering and then sharing the stories that, Apps says, go beyond the story that is recalled and told. Daloz (1986), who also wrote a book that was transformative for me, *Effective Teaching and Mentoring*, says that stories are important for adults, "for in the great tales lies the syntax of our lives, the form by which we make meaning of life's changes" (p. 22). Teachers and mentors use stories to provide a structure that followers can use to structure their own experiences. Stories can "reconnect things for us, place our fears in context, help us to see new forms of meaning" (p. 24). Stories, he says, take the readers on a journey, in a good direction. Daloz's narratives can be personal as when he shares a meeting with Emerald, a bookkeeper working in her brother's small sawmill, or iconic, as when he shares the story of story of Dante being led by his mentor Virgil. His stories about mentoring and transformation allow us to understand at a deeper level than scholarly, cognitive words might be able to uncover or elicit.

Sometimes, it is when writing a personal story that we understand our own transformation more profoundly. The following is an updated story I (Michael) wrote years ago and it helped me at the time to connect part of my past to where I was at the time I wrote it. I called it "You Can't Go Home Again".

I grew up in Kansas. My elementary school was Carter, in Wichita, Kansas and the family farm, where my sisters Mary and Amy, and my brother David, often spent the summer, was just outside Winfield, a few miles south.

A few years ago I had the opportunity to visit Wichita. I decided to visit our old home there, the first place I really remember, and the farm, where we had learned to drive, on a tractor; to swim, in the creek; to sing loud and without shame, in our little white church with a steeple; and to do all the myriad chores youngsters help with on a farm.

Years before on a trip I had tried to find our home in Olathe, Kansas, where I'd gone to high school. I remember combing the streets for hours. Olathe, a perfect little town of 20,000 when I'd lived there, had grown into another suburb of Kansas City. I thought at the time that sometimes you literally can't go home again. I was saddened by that realization.

Things change. Companies with which you thought you'd retire let you go or rearrange your career opportunities. Friends move on or move in to your life. A new interest captures your imagination. Children metamorph your world. You can't go back to what you once were.

Transformation is irreversible. You can't unlearn something or unexperience something or take back a thought. Once your mind is opened to new ways of looking at the world you can never go back to not-knowing. Once you've experienced life in a helpful or destructive way you are always changed you can never go back to not-having-experienced. Once you've felt joy, or peace, or pain, or pleasure, or angst, or fear you can never go back to "not-having-felt."

As I drove toward our little home in Wichita I wondered what it would be like. I remembered so many happy days, playing kick-the-can, roaming the streets, growing up. I turned onto the street and realized that although I had changed so much over 40 years, it had not. Perhaps it was just my mind playing games, but it seemed like it had deteriorated, become smaller. I didn't want to come home here again.

An hour later I was on a rural road approaching the old homestead, Grandview Ranch. My grandma had to sell it after grandpa died early. If you've ever had to sell your family farm you know the scars only cover a ripping apart of your soul from the land that never really heals. You can't go home again. You can't go back.

I stopped along the side of the road and reminisced about homemade ice cream and holding roman candles over the fields on Fourth of Julys past. I thought about my grandfather, and how he affects us still, years after his death. I remembered the time a horse reared up with my dad astride and fell back, the saddle horn gouging into his side. I remembered and I remembered.

The farm had changed, though, and so had I. The very dirt, of course, was different. My thoughts and hopes and perspectives had moved on, and as I pointed my camera over the hood of my car I realized it was good that I couldn't go home again. It could never be the same because I could never be the same. You can't go home again, I thought this time, looking out over beautiful Kansas farmlands, and I wouldn't want to.

Too many people I meet have a victim mentality—they wish for the past and believe someone has taken it away. They remember the old company fondly, forgetting that they complained about it at the time. They grouse about new technology, forgetting how much easier most things are these days.

When I was in Ireland a few years ago I visited, like many people do, the castles. It was a important insight for me to realize that the royalty of that era lived in circumstances that we today would consider impoverished and unhealthy in every way. Do you really want to go back home again?

The homes of our past reside within our souls. You can't go home again, because in the best of ways our home travels with us no matter where we go.

Although stories may be used in many ways, our task here is to talk about the use of stories to instruct or open up thinking rather than to constrain or limit it.

SUMMARY

I use stories in my workshops to derange student stories, to find new possibilities, and foster strangeness, irregularity, and non-linearity as much as to encourage revision and cleaning up after yourself...

Brian Kiteley, *The 3 a.m. Epiphany: Uncommon Writing Exercises*

That Transform Your Fiction (2005, p. 4)

In this chapter, we integrate transformative learning theory with storytelling. We explore how transformative learning and storytelling intersect; that is, how individuals can engage in transformative learning through the telling and reading of stories. When people tell stories, they are making meaning of their experiences through the telling. When people read stories, they are positioning themselves in the stories and gaining insights about their beliefs, values, and meaning perspectives. We illustrate these processes by calling on our own stories as well as important stories in our immediate history. We have learned that the result of transformative learning can be a deep shift in perspective, increase self-awareness and openness, and can give us sounder bases for the perspectives we hold. Stories have the power to instigate those outcomes.

The narratives in this book are included because they are stories of transformation told from different perspectives and from a variety of experiences. Our authors are not necessarily professional writers though we think you will find they tell their stories compellingly. So far we have discussed the basics of transformative learning (Chapter 1) and storytelling (Chapter 2) and how stories relate to transformative learning (this chapter). Next we share actual stories of transformation, told by those who have experienced transformative learning. We discuss each story and how it might be interpreted in light of transformative learning theory.

TRANSFORMATIVE LEARNING BASED ON PSYCHOLOGICAL DILEMMAS

Life is guided by a changing understanding of and interpretation of my experience. It is always in process of becoming.

Carl Rogers, *On Becoming a Person*, 1961, p. 27

This chapter focuses on transformative learning related to shifts in a learner's psychological meaning perspective, to use Mezirow's language. Psychological meaning perspectives are often formed in childhood and relate to constructs such as self-esteem, self-concept, fear, anxiety, and identity. In adulthood, when learners face a psychological dilemma such as illness or changing jobs, uncritically assimilated childhood perspectives are often called into question. We illustrate this process with two quite different stories. Art begins his story with his formative years as a child and the limited options that were available to him. He saw education and learning as a way to escape from the "survival options" existing in his rural Mexican village. As an adult, he had achieved the goals he set for himself as a child, but he was plagued by doubt and a nagging feeling that he was missing something in his life. Art made a major change in his life, but then he was hit with financial disaster as the economy collapsed. He needed to redefine his identity and his life.

Susan's story is like an inverted version of Art's story. Whereas Art started out life in an oppressive and limited context, Susan was protected and blessed as a child. She was the golden girl, a loved daughter, a champion competitive swimmer, and a person whose opportunities were unlimited. When she was home from college for the summer and swimming in a swimming hole in the river, she fell from a rope swing and broke her back. Susan's life changed forever. She redefined her identity and her life.

JUMPING INTO THE VOID – BY ART

As a little boy—some would say astute beyond my years or at least heartily creative—I saw only three ways to survive in the rural Mexican village where I was born. It was a matter of staying alive or finding a way out. My options were:

1. Drug dealer
   Drugs were a rampant business—visible and lucrative, even to my very young eyes.

2. Singer

I was blessed with an amazing voice, ear for music and penchant for performing. One of the only good things my father did was encourage my singing by hoisting me onto table tops at local bars and allowing me to lose myself in the joy of entertaining, if only for a few moments and to a half-listening crowd of *cerveza* drinking locals.

3. Field worker

My parents dragged me and my siblings to fields to harvest whatever was in season from sugarcane to sesame. I still carry the scars—scalding burns on my hands, crushed shoulders from the weight of the loads, and deformed feet from the tight boots and bone breaking labor.

The turning point in my young life was when I witnessed two drug dealers knifing each other in a bloody, savage fight in the village square. I remember the sound of metal on flesh, the flash of the blade, and the fear and fascination I saw in the eyes of the gathering crowd. I saw a man die that day which no little boy should have to see.

From that horrifying episode, a decision was made: option one was out of the question. The likely violence and loss of dignity, if not also of one's life, terrified me. I was only a child but I knew I wanted to be a father one day and I would not want that kind of life for my family nor to be that kind of role model. I loved life too much to risk truncating it for fast, dangerous money.

Music was still a possibility and dear to my heart. I felt real pride and pleasure when I sang my lungs out in front of the men gathered in the bars where my father went. I knew I had talent, but the hard faces and empty looks in the eyes of those men silently told me I had no future in the town. I could sing for my adoring mother at home but that was not going to earn us any money or help us in a concrete way.

Field work was how my family survived. My ten siblings and I—spanning more than 15 years in age—were packed into the bed of a pick-up truck, hauled across the country to Veracruz and back, stopping to harvest wherever we could find work. The small earnings we made did nothing to diminish the pain of the brutal physical work and the desperation we felt just to feed ourselves. Working in those fields for hours or days at a time posed its undeniable physical demands, but the mindless work allowed my brain to wander and my imagination to soar. It was a way for me to escape, if only in my mind. Eventually, I came up with a possible solution between one sesame stalk and another.

I chose to educate myself and to build my future one day at a time, like the slow growing process of the plants I plucked with my own hands. I was wise but not very patient. Once I made the decision, I wanted to get on with my life and find success elsewhere as soon as possible. I was not yet ten years old, but I felt I had—or should have—my eye squarely on the future. I was certain it was going to be a golden future and I wanted to get there fast. First goal: read as much as possible. I started gathering everything I could find with written words on it—discarded newspapers, magazines, advertisements, labels of products, the occasional book.

I kept my stash of words under my bed and would fish them out late at night. Even exhaustion from working outside all day could not keep me from my reading and learning. I called it "feeding my brain." I read by the light of a flame in a lamp I had built myself (my future as an engineer started to take form). While my vocabulary and knowledge were growing—I was like a sponge soaking up every word I could—this practice almost led to tragedy. One night as I read, I was in charge of rocking the cradle of my baby sister until she fell asleep. Somehow the flame of the lamp got too close to my papers and the string I had rigged up as a rocking device, and a fire broke out in the bedroom. My secret reading had put me and my family in grave danger. Fortunately, I was able to yell for help, and my extremely patient and forgiving mother doused the fire before anyone was hurt. I knew I had to get out faster. I could not risk hurting my family or myself, and would not let anything stand in my way.

Forty years later I find myself a successful businessman and engineer, a father, in my second marriage, feeling comfortable with hard earned financial freedom. Over twenty-five years with one company and decades of saving, I was a goal setter and I relished in achieving those goals, climbing one step at a time up the corporate ladder. I was constructing a solid nest egg to live on in my eventual retirement. It made me feel safe watching my bank account grow, numbers flipping upward each month. I would never allow myself to return to the dire economic situation of my youth.

In general, life was good. Business was good. My relationship with my wife was good. Mostly back on track after my tormented childhood and a long ago divorce, I had dedicated seven years getting into shape, both physical and mental, and preparing myself for the next strategic phase of my life. I was starting to learn to make room in my life for pleasure rather than constant work and fatigue. I admit I had workaholic tendencies, but mostly because I was passionate about my work as an engineer. I loved working with my hands, identifying and fixing problems, and being compensated for my efforts and accomplishments.

Although my career was moving along at a steady pace, from time to time there was a nagging feeling in the back of my mind. I could not say I was fully satisfied. I was moving in the right direction but not at the pace I would have liked. Always harsh on myself—in order to meet my goals—I wanted more and I wanted that larger success faster. Was it selfish of me to want more? Even with an occasional doubt, I recognized some certainties. I was not convinced I wanted to stay in the same job with the same company for many more years until retirement. I knew I could make that choice, meet the status quo and continue to cash my paychecks. But that was not enough to me anymore. I began to believe I was missing out on something more fulfilling. I could not accept that my current job would be my maximum achievement in life; even if I was proud of the work I did, I knew I was capable of much more and on a grander scale. A wave was pushing me ahead. It was time to make a move—now or never.

I told my manager that it was time for me to make a change. He was shocked and tried to dissuade me. My company had grown accustomed to my presence, my work ethic and willingness to take on new challenges, a tireless problem solver. Perhaps short sightedly, they had not planned for my departure. Managers, colleagues and peers tried to convince me to stay; it was not the time to leave. They threw me a curve ball—demanding I sign a non-competition/non-disclosure agreement—and they were stunned when I agreed to sign it. They challenged me with questions about what I would do outside the company. I did not have many clear answers yet, but something deep inside told me it was time to act. So I did. I took the leap and departed the company after many successful years. I jumped into a void and prayed that I would land on my feet. It was a risk, but one I felt I needed to make, (almost) regardless of the outcome. If we don't take risks once in a while, how do we know what else might be out there for us?

I had an urge to do different things each morning from those I had done for many years. I had the habit of sleeping only a few hours per night, and I looked forward to the chance to fill my time with new activities. I had been longing for some time to myself—to pursue painting, writing, traveling for pure pleasure—not for work. I could stoke my passion for music again. I wanted a chance to live, and not to define myself by the work I did. I had come to realize that life was not work, work was not life, despite the fact that for many years I had focused entirely, and perhaps too much, on work. I know that my health and relationships had suffered from that obsession. Something in me clicked like a light switch; it was time to make amends—mostly with myself—and to change the trajectory of my future.

My transition into my new life started February 2008. For the next few months, I enjoyed the activities I had foreseen—art, music, exercise, literature, time with my wife, time to myself. It was a time of replenishment for me, my body and mind—in anticipation of my next challenge and adventure yet to be determined.

June 2008 arrived and one morning I woke up to find my bank accounts frozen, my investment accounts inaccessible, my ATM cards non-functioning. I had twenty dollars in my pocket, and rent was due. The U.S. banking crisis had crashed into my life. I panicked; I knew I had ample funds in the bank to live on but I could not access any of them. No one had answers at the banks I called; no one could provide information or guarantee that I would see my money again. **Helpless** is not strong enough a word to describe my feeling at that moment. Frightened, lost, abruptly adrift with no anchor. For someone like me who relies on and believes strongly in planning, this situation was inexplicable. I was the professional who fixed problems for companies, but now I faced one of the biggest personal problems of my life.

Luckily, I was not a person who focused too much or too long on the negative, nor allowed myself to lose control. I knew I had to fight through the problem. I would not let it destroy me. I was extremely fortunate to have by my side my supportive and clear-headed wife. She usually did not mince words and this time was no different. When I told her what was going on, she looked me square in the eyes and told me to get a grip. She said, "Look at you—all the schooling, all the experience you have. You have overcome problems before and you will again. You can do anything you want. I'll help you do whatever you want to do." She too had lost some savings in the crash, and it was a blow to her psyche as it had been to mine. But, together, we knew we would recover—as individuals and as a pair. The losses would hurt for a while. We had no choice but to start saving again.

I was without a job and had lost a big chunk of my savings; my wife still had her job as an educator and some savings. Eventually we were able to access some of our funds and were thankful for what we had left. Nevertheless, the loss of many tens of thousands of dollars from one day to the next caused certain pain and desperation. It is a bruise I will probably feel all my life, like the physical ones I inherited from the fields—but the transition of the recovery process made me stronger and wiser.

It was to be expected that I would feel sorry for myself. I questioned what I believed in—God, science, time, humanity, space. I am both a scientist and artist—I found myself challenging all angles of my knowledge. I remembered people, like some in my childhood town, who chose to stay downtrodden or deprived without ever attempting to reach a brighter place—geographic or personal. They were ironically content with the sadness and hardship of their circumstances. I didn't want to be that kind of person. I had escaped that life before and I was in the process of doing it again. I preferred to be the person who others might call reckless, too ambitious, maybe arrogant in my reactions and endeavors. Occasional failure is bound to happen and at times necessary for us to open our eyes to new awareness and opportunities.

Both in science and art, movement is imperative, change is certain. I was living a time of transition—like I had many times before—from childhood, to manhood, to leaving my country and my job, to rebounding from sudden financial struggle, to getting on with my life.

TRANSFORMATION FOLLOWING A TRAUMATIC DISABILITY – BY SUSAN STUNTZNER, ASSISTANT PROFESSOR, UNIVERSITY OF IDAHO – COEUR D'ALENE

Growing up, I was the youngest of two children. During my formative years, my parents and family taught me the importance of setting goals; doing my best at whatever I did; working hard; living the best life I can; planning for the future; and being an honest, caring, and considerate person. Within this environment, I felt safe and, in hindsight, protected from some of the harsh realities of life. This protection did not mean I knew nothing about difficulties as I sure had my own set of "life" experiences growing up. For instance, I remember several times being picked on and made fun of by the 'class bully' or unkind peers, falling off my bicycle several times – one of which resulted in a hospitalization because I hit my head on the curb, and learning how to win and lose a race with dignity. But at that time, these were experiences kids had, right? Maybe yes. Maybe no, but they were *my* experiences.

During this time, at the age of four, my parents enrolled me on swim team. When I started, my sister had gone before me; however, I had the extra bonus of having an affinity for water, despite my best interests. One of those situations involved wandering off from the neighborhood and finding my way to the newest-built plush motel and standing on the side of the motel's swimming pool acting as if I was going to get in. While I have no recollection of this particular experience, it is a story well-known within my family and I believe it served as one of the motivators to put me onto the swim team.

For the next 15 years, I swam competitively in AAU swimming, and overall, it was a wonderful experience. Beyond learning how to swim, I learned many other invaluable lessons and skills which continue to hold value and I still draw upon when life gets tough. For instance, I learned more about setting goals, commitment, dedication, hard work, determination, winning and losing, and feeling good about my own progress regardless of the race's outcome. While all these are great lessons to have and attributes to develop as a part of life, it was a little bit later that I came to see how all of these skills would be used as the foundation for an ever-changing life experience.

Following my sophomore year in college, I was home for the summer, working as a life guard. One day after my morning job, a friend and I went up the river about 25 miles. It was a beautiful sunny and warm day. My friend and I were swimming at a local swimming hole for about an hour, when I fell off a rope swing and landed on the river's bank. Within seconds, my legs were tingling and numb – I "intuitively" knew I broke my back. As I laid there, my friend went to get some help and because of my lifeguard training, I knew not to let anyone touch or move me. Before the day was out, I was flown to a rehabilitation hospital up North heading for surgery. The doctor told my parents and I that I would likely be paralyzed from the waist down and not walk again.

What unfolded from this experience was the start of transformation following disability. While I knew people had disabilities, I was not aware of the challenges reported and often experienced by them. No one told me that persons with disabilities were viewed as "incapable" and as "second-class" citizens, treated inadequately and poorly by society and persons without a disability, viewed as unattractive or undesirable relationship partners, and were the recipients of much social stigma and biases. Boy, was I in for a surprise! I just did not know it yet.

In the coming days, months, and years, a beautiful change began. I came to see my spinal cord injury as an essential element of my own process of transformation and as a journey that provided me with many opportunities for change, growth, and transcendence. With that said, the early stages following my injury were 'life-altering' as my internal process set me on a new and unforeseen path. During the first four weeks, I remember having a major epiphany. I was still in the hospital, not yet walking or doing much of anything, although I was starting to demonstrate initial signs of muscle return. I spent a lot of time thinking about what my life had been like up until the point of my injury and what it might be like in the future. I had so many questions and so much information I wanted to know.

One day, I realized there was no going back to my "old life." No matter how I looked at it, I understood I could not jump the divide or return to that part of life I once knew. I remember visualizing myself standing at a "fork in the road." On the right side of the fork was the path of my previous life. On the left was my new path, that of a person with a disability. This new path was perceived as one which afforded me with many new learning opportunities and experiences, and numerous unknowns yet to be revealed. Although I could not walk and I had no idea of what my future held, I felt hopeful, energized, and eager. I wanted to do everything within my power to become as independent as possible to create a life worth living, despite the *odds* or the outcome projected by medical staff.

I remember thinking my new path would give me many opportunities to learn about myself, my abilities, my sense of inner strength, and life lessons that were miles beyond those of my same-aged peers. Rather quickly, I became more invested in the outcome of my career choice and direction, especially given the fact that I had to consider occupations and choices which utilized my intelligence and mental faculties as these would become my greatest assets. I felt a sense of reassurance or "intuitive knowing" that life would be just fine and if I could deal well with this situation, I could probably overcome and move beyond most anything life had to offer.

Over the next two months, I was discharged from the hospital and walking with below-the-knee, ankle foot orthotics and a walker. I returned to my hometown and participated in physical therapy two to four times per week and tested my physical abilities and limitations through a trial-and-error process. For instance, I took my walker, by myself, and strived to walk a mile two to three times a week. To the onlooker, it probably looked painful or tedious. But not to me! I was ecstatic that I could stand and walk on any level; something the medical staff told me I would probably never achieve. Adding to my new-found delight was the recognition of my physical therapists that my physical abilities *defied* the logic of textbooks. They shared with me that they did not understand how I was able to do what I do with the muscle strength that I had, because it was not medically possible according to their formalized knowledge. Not really sure how to *process* that information, I simply felt grateful and blessed. It was like I had a second chance at life and it was up to me to continue on my path and to make the most of my life and my abilities. I had a sense that the rest would be revealed in due time. My responsibility was to stay the course.

As time passed and for several years, I faced and endured numerous challenges. The most difficult was recognizing, dealing with, accepting, and moving beyond other peoples' negative attitudes, unkind words and behaviors, and societal biases toward persons with disabilities. This is the part of living with a disability where some, myself included, recognize and "see" the unkind side of humanity—the side that most people would say, "That doesn't happen. That is not real." Well the truth is, it does happen, and it is real. Most persons without a disability don't rub shoulders with discrimination or these types of social justices because there is not any visible or perceived difference that sets them apart from mainstream America. Such experiences represent the private side or unheard voice of living with a disability, and when continued, promote additional social marginalization.

Looking back, I was not mentally or emotionally prepared for these experiences and for the first five years, I spent a lot time trying to maneuver other peoples' discomfort and unkind interactions. I remember thinking, "If I just find the right equation, other people will feel comfortable and I can give them the right answer." Despite my intentions and commitment to put others at ease, there were no easy answers or identifiable equations. Each situation had to be dealt with and approached on a case-by-case basis. This set of experiences was another opportunity of transformative understanding, desired or not. Because of my new reality, I was now faced with the task of how to integrate my previous world view of life and fairness with my experiences of disability, the knowledge of others' discomfort and lack of acceptance, and my self-identity and self-concept.

Although difficult, the "collective" of these experiences have taught me to focus on the positive ways my life changed and on the wonderful lessons I learned about myself. For instance, I learned to accept and value myself and all that I am regardless of what others think or perceive. I am much more confident and secure because of my disability and life experiences. I am not afraid to try new things. I have learned a great deal about tenacity, perseverance, and staying the course. I know, today, I have a choice in how I will respond to others' un-pleasantries, and I am only responsible for my own actions and decisions—I do not have to absorb other peoples' negativity or fears. I know that given a choice, I would not change a thing about having a visible condition.

Living with a disability has also given me numerous opportunities to live life to the fullest, some of which include: going to graduate school and obtaining my PhD, traveling abroad to other countries, meeting the Dali Lama, educating professionals about disability, and working in a profession I absolutely love! All of these experiences have unveiled the many ways God has used my experience to benefit and help others and for that I am very blessed!

Living life well following disability has, indeed, been a transformation. This experience encompasses over 28 years of my life and has changed my beliefs, perspectives, world view, and feelings about myself as well as my understanding of disability. While I do not remember having any negative feelings about disability, growing up, it was a situation that people did not talk about. Students with very severe disabilities were usually pulled-out and rarely integrated; thus, my peers and I were not exposed to the realities of persons with disabilities or to opportunities that could shape our understanding. Today, I understand that even when unspoken, such actions send messages about disability, as well as beliefs and expectations of persons with disabilities. At the very least, separating persons with disabilities from their peers promotes the continued tolerance of misunderstanding the abilities and capabilities of persons with disabilities.

Today, I am grateful for the learning, growing, and transforming opportunities bestowed upon me because of my disability. While they were oftentimes not easy, many of them have molded me into the person I am today – someone who is complete, appreciative, compassionate, open-minded, caring, and creative. I am afforded the gift of viewing life from multiple perspectives and I understand how living life on the left fork in the road turned out better than I could have imagined. Who would have ever guessed?

COMMENTARY

What is striking about Art's and Susan's stories is the optimism and positive responses they both had to very difficult situations—one being a seemingly impossible beginning to life in a context where opportunities and options were so limited, and one being an equally seemingly impossible life-changing accident. This makes us wonder about the extent to which hope, optimism, and courage play a role in transformative learning. Other individuals in these same circumstances may have dropped into a swamp of despair and hopelessness. We return to this question in our discussion in Chapter 9.

Both stories have to do with reshaping and redefining identity. As a child, Art could see himself as a drug dealer, a singer, or a field worker, but he rejected those identities and found another identity that took him out of his childhood context. This, in itself, makes a good story, but Art did not stop there. He paid attention to his "nagging feeling" and looked for another way to understand himself and another way to be in the world. Even when he was thrown off this path by financial disaster, he quickly rallied and created a detour around the obstacle placed in his path.

Susan was forced into an equally dramatic identity shift. She went from being a successful competitive athlete to being a person with a spinal cord injury. She not only had to deal with this change in who she was, but she also had to learn to understand and accept others' views of a person with a physical disability. Susan realized she could never go back to her earlier life, and she found joy in her new life and her new identity.

We know that experiencing a psychological dilemma can call uncritically assimilated childhood perspectives into question and has the potential to lead to transformative learning. What we do not really know is how and why this happens. It is our hope that through the reading and interpreting of stories, we can gain some insights into this question. We continue with this quest in the next chapters.

TRANSFORMATION IN RESPONSE TO LOSS AND TRAUMA

> Where you used to be, there is a hole in the world, which I find myself constantly walking around in the daytime, and falling in at night.

Edna St. Vincent Millay, *Letters of Edna St. Vincent Millay*, 1972, p. 102

In this chapter, we focus on transformative learning that involves a response to loss and trauma in a person's life. We explore this phenomenon in relation to trauma encountered in adulthood and the role that educators may play in both informal and formal settings in helping others cope with grief and tragedy. Research shows that transformative learning is often a result of loss and trauma; for example, Cranton, Taylor, & Stuckey (2012) found that 43 out of 136 participants described personal loss and trauma as the event that provoked their transformative learning experience. We illustrate this process with a story related to the death of a parent and the parallel spouse's story about the same death and, secondly, a story related to the trauma of a serious illness.

Alyssa's story is complex in that it consists of layers of loss. Her father died, but this is only the beginning of her story. She then turns to the transformation she witnessed in her mother's reaction to her father's death, and from there, her story turns to her own transformative learning in relation to her mother's story.

Laurence's story is about his response to a life-changing illness. At first glance, one would think that Laurence's story belongs with Susan's story (Chapter 4), but we responded to a subtle difference between the two stories. Susan's accident and the resulting spinal cord injury led her to a psychological dilemma—a change in her identity from athlete and a competitive swimmer to a disabled person. Laurence's story is a response to trauma—an illness—and, as a result, he makes important changes in his lifestyle and eating habits, but he does not see himself as a more fully-realized person. To use Mezirow's language, Laurence experienced a disorienting dilemma, and this led him to critically question and revise his perspectives about his eating habits and, more broadly, his frame of reference about the mind-body relationship.

OPENING THE DOORS OF TRANSFORMATION – BY ALYSSA NOTA

My childhood memories are filled with sounds—the creaking roof on windy autumn nights, the squeak of the kitchen utensils drawer, the roar of NFL game crowds late on Monday night TV, and my father closing the heavy sliding glass doors in the living room before going to bed on summer nights.

One night, a few months after my father passed away, I noticed something different. My mother was sleeping with the doors open. (No one had pulled the heavy glass doors shut; instead, the silky screen door stood almost invisible against the night. Cool New England breezes were welcome to enter, mosquitoes less so.)

As a daughter who had inherited her father's exact personality and routines, among other things, my first instinct was to close the heavy doors, shut them up tight. My hand on the wooden door handle, my nose inches from the screen, the smell of green and life reaching me, something caught my attention—peace and quiet of the thick starry night—and a calm came over me. I knew my mom was going to be fine. Although we all missed my dad and felt his absence daily, I knew everything was going to be ok. We all slept with the doors open that night.

As daughters are often enamored with their fathers at any age, I was too... and never saw my father as ill or weak; rather, he was a noble hero, a giant in my eyes—and not only for his towering height. One would have never known the serious medical issues he dealt with for many decades of his life. This story, though, is not about him or the special tacit understanding we had – two quiet people with an uncanny similarity of looks, personality and way of being.

Rather, this story is about the transformation I witnessed in my mother after my father's death. More than a personal change in her, it was an enlightening change in the way I saw my mother.

Women can tell so many stories of transformation and transition in their lives— nature and time take their course and leave their own trail of transformations. At other times it is the woman herself who makes the changes, through her own choice or volition. A line on one's face, a silver streak in one's hair—inevitable traces of time we can choose to accept or to compete against with varying measures and emotions. Inevitable, however, is the finiteness and impermanence of life—and therefore, of our loved ones and ourselves. Life throws itself at us in its exasperating complexity—at times offering us a chance to choose, at others giving us no recourse or escape.

Over the course of a lifetime, as females we confront many potential changing roles: daughter, sibling, girlfriend, wife, partner, mother, caregiver.... Changing bodies, changing looks, changing jobs and responsibilities, changing sense of beauty and style.... Changes are many more in number than the years we live.

The change/transition from "wife to widow" is one I had never considered (as a girl turned married woman now in my early 40's)—until my father passed away and I saw my mother in a different light. I had never considered her role as "wife" before, and now could not even begin to understand what it meant to have lost one's spouse of over 45 years. "Widow" was a heavy word in my vocabulary, as if it possessed great physical weight like an unwieldy wool coat—and I was not ready to burden my mother with it.

I was one of the lucky ones who had parents who adored and respected each other and were a constant, solid pair. I am sure they had their disagreements—as in any relationship—but they perfectly kept those moments private and away from the eyes of their three children—my brothers and I. The youngest of the three, perhaps I got to spend more time living with them both, particularly after my two older brothers got married and moved on with their careers and families. I always saw my parents as a unified pair, a unified force at home. Coincidentally, also in work they were unified: they taught at neighboring high schools, and as such, drove to school together each morning for close to 30 years. As a child one often does not recognize the value of one's parents, nor of the limited time they have to share with their children and each other.

When asked at an administrative office for the date their marriage ended, my mother said to the clerk, incensed, "It did not end, it will never end…." That is the kind of marriage and timeless connection my parents had…and have. Loyalty and fidelity were unspoken rules and tenets of their relationship. Some would say theirs was a marriage "of other times" or "other generations" but, in my opinion, they are a model for any age and type of relationship. My mother's constancy and commitment—to her husband and family—are enviable qualities. After my father's death, her commitment did not wane, but surprised me by extending further to embrace even more of life and the people in it: relatives, friends—old and new, community, church, health, wellness, hobbies, entertainment, causes she believed in…. She was filled by a new energy and drive of which I had previously seen only a part.

As a result, it was not until my father passed away that I saw my mother as an individual, her own person, her own being. It was both fascinating and slightly disconcerting at the same time—not as alarming as if seeing a stranger in my living room, but rather seeing someone familiar with different eye or hair color. A considerable change had taken place when I had least expected it. Maybe this awakening would have happened anyway with age—but I am not certain. Do daughters get to a point where they see their mothers as equals—in the sense of "two women" versus "one mother and one daughter"? Where is that point in the continuum of a lifetime—or in the separate lives of mother and daughter? Is there an eventual moment when the two lines converge?

My mother had dedicated the majority of her life to caring for her husband and children, all while working full time, never missing a child's sports game or school event, providing full-circle support to her family—birthdays, holidays and, more importantly, every normal day in between. Without children of my own, I know I could not have done what she did all those years. How she purposefully, gracefully juggled all those elements is beyond me.

I suppose, in our relationship, I had always identified myself as "daughter," and my mother as "parent." My father's death reshuffled those cards—and in doing so, added the identities of woman, companion, the closest of relatives united in the loss of our loved one, but much more than that; there always remained "mother" and "parent" and "daughter." In my mind it is right and true that a mother is always a mother, and a daughter is always a daughter. I have a hard time believing in those mother-daughter pairs who claim to be "best friends" or "equals"—to me, a parent is always a parent and that relationship is sacred and important; that role cannot be replaced or taken away. It can transform, but the basic elements remain the same. The strength, support, stability, *structure* that a parent—a *good* parent—gives to his or her child is irreplaceable, irrefutable. My brothers and I are immensely fortunate to have received that gift of structure, within the profound context of a happy home life, childhood and family: a gift from both our parents.

So the transition I experienced was not a change in relationship or role, as much as a new view of my mother, and perhaps also of myself as her daughter, both of us in a new phase of our lives—as women, as human beings.

At my father's funeral service I felt a surge of energy, like I had to do something. So when it came time for one of the readings, I knew I had to do it, for my father but also for my entire family. I was no longer the little sister—I was now someone who could help soothe the pain of my family at a difficult moment. So I stood up with my husband and together we read sections of what my mother had chosen. I read a passage from Shakespeare about goodness, fairness, nobility of person and spirit. I am grateful and proud to have found that strength. After the service, my mother said, "Alyssa is the strongest one of us all." I was proud to know my mother thought that, and to know that I could stand up and take care of my family when it was needed.

My mom's transformation—or perhaps reversion to herself, a self I had never known or been smart enough to notice—has been eye-opening for me. To know how heartbroken she is—but to see her go on, to continue her life not only the best she can but fully and colorfully/ vividly—to pursue dreams and interests, to set new goals and plans, to move ahead, enjoying her time with family, friends, and also alone …. I saw her stepping cautiously, then more confidently into this next phase of her life. She started taking classes she was interested in, going to movies with friends, reading more books in a week than a speed-reading critic, swimming at the local pool, filling her time and her spirit with new, or perhaps temporarily cast-aside, favorite activities. I saw her spirit filling with the satisfaction of the things that she had purposely chosen to put aside for most of her life in order to take care of me, my brothers and our father. I saw her coming back into herself. I was (and am) very proud of her, and knew she was stronger than I, no matter what she said.

She proved she can be comfortable in her solitude, but also active and busy with her friends. Her group of women friends is amazing—an immensely powerful source of support and strength—and she notes that often to anyone who will listen. She credits her friends with helping her to get through every day. They are women of all ages—mostly over 65—who have had life experiences of all kinds and share the details daily over coffee. Marriages, divorces, children, grandchildren, losses, accidents, illnesses—but more often, inspiring stories of quotidian or long-fought successes, study, travel, growth, learning, professionalism and pioneering careers in nursing, education and business at pivotal historic moments when women did not always have the freedoms and access that we do today. Lots of laughter fills those mornings, and every day they leave each other re-energized and motivated to move ahead again—if only until the next coffee—and story-filled morning meeting.

These women, including my mother, are inspirational in their drive, humor, friendship, wherewithal, steadfastness... They are strong in numbers, stronger in dignity. For some, constancy may be a personal attribute or a purposeful choice, while transformation is inevitable. My mother taught me that sometimes we choose the moment to learn and grow, and sometimes life chooses the moment for us.

FALLING INTO TRANSFORMATION - BY LAURENCE ROBERT COHEN

One day, I fell. That must be understood, "or nothing wonderful can come of the story I am going to relate" like Marley being very dead in the *Christmas Carol*. Being dead was an absolute state for Marley and his death absolute for Scrooge as well which led him deep into a transformative Christmas Eve and a transformed life. I fell very far. My falling came as an absolute as well. Falling opened me into a long transformative moment, and later on, it led me to another transformative understanding.

When I say, "I fell," I mean that not as some clumsy tripping and stumbling to the ground. That sort of falling would have come as a relief. Falling for me was a complete dissolution of the world, of the universe and my physical place in that world and in that universe. It's the kind of thing that gets your attention. It certainly got mine.

At thirty-five, I went back to college at Arizona State University. It had only taken twenty years to figure out that idea had some merit, and that was transformative in its own way. But that's another story. It felt like such a good idea, I continued into a Master's in an Interdisciplinary Humanities program. I was learning and teaching which as an early high school dropout was another transformation and yet another story. My studies made sense to me, and my teaching held great adventure and even more meaning for me. In short, everything in life felt as if it were going very, very well.

Then I fell.

Sometime before, I went through a rather mild flu, but my left ear still seemed stuffed and slightly deaf. It bothered some, but I thought it would just pass. It didn't pass. It arrived full blown. I was crossing an open space on campus on my way to someplace, which has faded in the light of what happened. All of a sudden, my left ear filled up and emptied out. I felt odd, ill, and needing attention. I was near the campus infirmary and managed to get into a back door a nurse opened for me when she saw my face and guessed my immediate need. I came in, and she took one look at me and grabbed the glasses off my face. Anything like direction, location, position, orientation, situation, even sensation, completely collapsed and then disappeared.

I fell.

My disorientation felt so complete that I scarcely knew when I hit the ground, and hit the ground I did, like someone who had been hit by a very large, very heavy bat or had simply died on his feet. Indeed, when they picked me up to get me off the floor where I took up needed space, even I felt that I was a dead weight. Indeed, I felt nearly dead. Death passed when I felt an explosive need to vomit. Vomiting tends to indicate a clear sign of life. Someone provided a receptacle and off I went. I lay back down and still felt ill. I tried to open my eyes, and the world spun in ways I never even considered possible. I felt sicker and broke into a cold sweat. Even writing about it now rather exhausts me. Then I had to defecate and urinate, and I couldn't keep it in. Some staff somehow got me to a bathroom and rather held me up when they sat me down. Off I went. They returned me to an examining table. A doctor asked me to open my eyes: "Your eyes are spinning around." In that the world was also spinning, I accepted his diagnosis or observation (Have you ever noticed that doctors often tell us what we already know and call it a diagnosis?). I just closed my eyes again and wondered if this would ever end this side of death.

Death did not come, and I eventually got back on my feet. The doctor told me he couldn't tell me what I wanted him to tell me—what was wrong. I could walk, but I felt moderately unsteady and disoriented in a way I hadn't known before. It wasn't like being drunk or any intoxication of the kind. It certainly wasn't funny. It wasn't fun. It wasn't much of anything but feeling out of sorts, out of time, out of touch, and very near tears. I didn't feel transformed. Maybe I felt translated into a language I didn't understand. It occurred to me that I might have just experienced a prelude to death.

Mundanely, I experienced something different: a craving for pretzels. I bought a small packet and ate them with pleasure, the saltiness especially satisfying. It was a favorite snack, if not the only one, and I suppose it felt like comfort food. I wasn't very comforted, but I felt it was the right thing to do. My ear was making a noise, not a ringing but a kind of electronic buzzing. I couldn't hear as well as I had. I tried to talk to friend about the incident, but I kept crying when I tried to describe it, so I gave up and went home.

I lay down and discovered the world wasn't exactly spinning, but it didn't feel really stable, and I felt slightly disoriented, almost dizzy but not quite. That's the way I stayed, more or less, both physically, mentally, and emotionally. I experienced more tears and, even more to my chagrin, anger as I went about the tasks of my life as a graduate student: attending classes, teaching classes, experiencing vertigo, and seeing doctors.

Finally, I went to a doctor who said there were two possibilities given these symptoms. It was either an incurable but not fatal disease called Meniere's or an inoperable tumor which was generally fatal. I would have the test the next day, and she would get an immediate reading to tell me the outcome. No waiting.

I waited that night knowing that my fate, melodramatic but quite true, hung in the balance, another cliché, but there we are. It works.

The test went off quite well, and it turned out to be the lesser of two evils: Meniere's disease. Thank you Monsieur Meniere—maybe. Maybe not. The incidents continued and the deafness moved in to stay as did the tinnitus. Sometimes the noise in my head woke me up in the middle of the night, so I could look around for what was wrong. There was something wrong, but it was in my head not in the world around me. Although I saw another doctor who experimented with some vitamins and supplements, everything went on unchanged. My life was changing because of all of these symptoms, and the doctor warned me I could even end up disabled. Some people killed themselves rather than live with this thing. I understood their point of view.

One fortuitous day, I was in the infirmary getting checked by a semi-retired doctor who attended medical conferences in his very spare time. He wanted to talk to me because he had heard something about Meniere's disease. He heard it unofficially in the hall during a break, but he assured me that's where most of what he learned at conferences happened. Another doctor found that when some of his patients with Meniere's reduced their salt intake, the symptoms got better. He didn't know why, but it happened.

I wanted it to happen to me. Without the slightest hesitation, I told the doctor that if I didn't have to go through the disabling vertigo and all the rest I didn't need to eat another grain of salt, not a scintilla of sodium, in my life. He thought that might be hard. I said it was more than a fair trade. I never intentionally ate salt again, and I have experienced a Meniere's incident only once in the past twenty–five years. What a bargain.

This choice transformed the way I saw food in my life and what food meant to my life in general. In that way, it transformed my life in ways I could not have imagined.

As someone born into the Western world, I received the Platonic—Descartian mind body meaning perspective as part of my formula of life. My mind and body were not of the same stuff, and the stuff of mind had the right and the power to command the stuff of body, and the body would do as it was told. It had better. I didn't know that I knew this, but I knew it as an essential and unquestioned, unquestionable truth of life. In some interesting way, it gives our ego, our sense of identity a certain kind of power that no one can take away. No matter how bereft we are in life, we feel that power over our bodies and can express it in any number of ways. One way the mind commands the body comes in what food the mind decides it wants and it tells the body that's what it has to have, what it has to like, even love by way of food. In that way, like many if not most people, I ate when I felt like, it, what I felt like, and often paid little attention to what I ate so long as it kept me going. That's what my mind told my body to accept.

At forty, I came face to face with a critical moment. My body was telling my mind what it had to do in order for both to survive. I might have eaten to survive before, but my mind did the ordering as to what. Now my body spoke up rather forcefully and offered a different form of survival and a different form of thinking about my mind and body, a different way of thinking about food in relationship to them. I could not deny that the Meniere's episodes upset my body.

Another ancillary meaning perspective I faced and resolved came in how I referred to symptoms of Meniere's. Typically, we call such things "attacks." The violence of the language simply upset me more emotionally and psychologically. That's my body doing the attacking, and so my mind perceives the body as an enemy. That didn't help. I didn't want war. I wanted peace and balance. At first, I used "incident," but I changed it here to "episode" to reflect the duration of the effects of such an experience. Language has power. I wanted that power to help not hinder my healing.

I could not deny that those same episodes upset, quite literally, my mind as well. I also thought about how my mind craved salt after the first episode. I felt satisfied when I ate the pretzels, but it also was bringing me to the next episode. I remembered how people had long told me about foods they loved but that also made them ill. They laughed at the difficulty, and they generally went right on getting hives or crabby or heartburn from eating that same food. The mind says "I want," and the body just has to accept it. Meniere's spoke too loudly for that, at least for me. These critical episodes told me that my mind and my body worked together to make a life, and the staff of that life, as people have said, was the food I chose to eat for mind and body.

Now my mind needed to encompass what it meant to take salt out of diet and body. It meant a very expansive set of choices in not just eating but living, but those choices seemed quite small compared to the size and scope of the Meniere's episodes. Salt didn't mean just the stuff we sprinkle on our food. It meant sodium in all its forms, which, I found, was everywhere. Based on the choice at hand, giving up all processed foods, in actual fact all foods prepared outside my home, the life of my mind needed to make new choices as well. It gave me my life back, and I welcomed the new perspectives or imperatives I felt about my body and the food my mind and body shared. The sickness and horror of Meniere's brought me to a place of realization and that to a transformation of my mind/body perspective that has lasted for all my life since that time.

It also led me into another confusion and realization and transformation. I met others who suffered from Meniere's. I would tell my story briefly, and I expected that these other sufferers would greet what I communicated as a joyful liberation and even salvation. I was wrong. Many times I heard people tell me that they couldn't give up salt or some food or other that contained salt. The first and most memorable for some reason was this: "I couldn't give up feta cheese." I gave up falling down, becoming violently ill, profoundly disoriented, and possibly disabled, and she couldn't give up feta cheese for all that. It didn't make sense to my previous mind/body meaning perspective let alone my newly revised one.

My desire for survival was very immediate and very demanding, so I made my choice: no salt and all that went with it. Others found their survival in keeping hold of an identity, possessing themselves as an identity in some way and that identity was deeply attached to salt, sodium, and the cornucopia of products and relationships that come with them. I felt no trouble in giving up Meniere's by forgetting salt. Others felt they would forget themselves, cease to be the same identity and, in that way, lose the survival of their identity, a thing entirely of mind. They would suffer a profound loss of health to hold fast to that identity. This forms part of the tragic nature of meaning perspectives in many situations. They create a situation where any other perspective, any other choice seems, and therefore becomes, impossible. Living out this tragic paradox of identity and survival has meant that people I have known and cared for would even eat themselves to death in one way or another.

I had fallen into understanding another meaning perspective, one that drove some people I have known to violate their bodily well-being for identity gratification. As the modern cliché goes, a meaning perspective can be something "to die for."

COMMENTARY

Here, we have two seemingly different stories, but each one illustrating a similar process. Alyssa's father died. She says, "As a daughter who had inherited her father's exact personality and routines my first instinct was to close the heavy doors, shut them up tight." She acknowledges that her father was her hero. And then she quickly turns to telling the story of her mother's reaction to her father's death. She grapples with the "wife to widow" transition that her mother experienced, and she writes, "As a result, it was not until my father passed away, that I saw my mother as an individual, her own person, her own being. It was both fascinating and slightly disconcerting at the same time—not as alarming as if seeing a stranger in my living room, but rather seeing someone familiar with different eye or hair color." It is this statement that brings us back to Alyssa's transformation, one that she spoke little of in her story. Her meaning perspective related to her mother had changed.

Laurence was walking through life in an ordinary way. He had returned to school as an adult, aged 35. Then he fell down. And this led to a series of events that led him to a medical diagnosis of Meniere's disease. As mentioned in the opening of the chapter, this experience led him to critically question his ideas about what he ate—a central component of how we see ourselves. Perhaps as significantly, his frame of reference about the mind-body relationship was revised as he considered how one affects the other. The body doesn't, he came to realize, just do what the mind demands. The body can also make demands to which the mind must respond in order to remain or to become healthy. Although he doesn't say it, this revised frame of reference might affect his perspective of the mind-body relationship beyond the eating of salt or even food to a broader array of health-related perspectives. We might ask whether this revision of Laurence's views about his change in diet and was also a revision of his identity, but there does not seem to be enough evidence of this. He made a conscious choice to eat in a more healthy manner, but this was not central to who he was. Laurence did not ever see himself as a "diseased person." Laurence went on to generalize his experience to others' decisions about how they eat.

Loss and trauma is clearly a way that individuals are led to transformative learning. Loss is usually defined as the loss of a loved one, but it can also be the loss of a job, or the loss of a way of life through illness. Alyssa's and Laurence's stories illustrate these two aspects of the meaning of loss.

CHAPTER 6

TRANSFORMATION THROUGH EDUCATIONAL EXPERIENCES

Passion, hope, doubt, fear, exhilaration, weariness, colleagueship, loneliness, glorious defeats, hollow victories, and, above all, the certainties of surprise and ambiguity – how can one begin to capture the reality of teaching in a single word or phrase?

Stephen D. Brookfield, *The Skillful Teacher*, 1990, p. 1

In this chapter, we present stories related to educational experiences. The origin of transformative learning theory lies in higher education (Mezirow, 1978), and since that time, the role that higher education plays in facilitating transformative learning has been a subject of considerable study (Kasworm & Bowles, 2012). Jose's story begins with the moment where he is just about to receive his master's degree, then goes back to trace the rocky journey involved in reaching this goal. Nayoung's story of Sung's transformation occurs in an alternative school in South Korea but begins when he reconnects, at age 16, with his mother.

Both of the stories in this chapter emphasize the role of the relationships between learner and educator in the process of transformative learning. Jose's parole officer believed in him and helped him become engaged in a dental assistant program. Jose also encountered Peter who founded a program that helps juveniles and young adults disengage and exit gangs. But it was when he enrolled in college and met a psychology professor who became his mentor and friend that his life really turned around. Sung's perspective is dramatically shifted by his relationship with others in his group and especially his relationship with an adult educator, Nayoung, who tells his story. The role of relationships in transformative learning has become increasingly acknowledged as scholars study the process (Taylor & Snyder, 2012). Relationships support and foster transformative learning, but connections between family members, spouses, and community members can also be challenged as people change. For example, in a classic movie, *Educating Rita*, a young hairdresser goes back to school, and the resulting transformation upset long standing relationships with her spouse and friends. Novels and movies often explore how relationships change—sometimes with great loss sometimes with great gain—when individuals grow. The role of mentors, teachers, coaches, parents and others who support a person's growth has long been acknowledged as an important factor in facilitating transformative learning.

Meaning perspectives are usually uncritically assimilated in childhood. We see this phenomenon in Sung's story, as told by Nayoung. Sung appears to engage in transformative learning prior to adulthood. Roger Gould (1978), who was an early influence on Mezirow, writes about the assumptions individuals form early in their lives from parents and early experiences about themselves and the world which might have been helpful at the time they were formed but which do not serve them well in adulthood.

Transformative learning is an adult learning theory because it involves the *transformation* of assumptions about oneself and the world. This is in contrast to the initial *formation* of those assumptions, which occurs in younger years as we come to believe "This is who I am" and "This is the world we live in." By definition, a person cannot transform something until it has been formed, and so this theory naturally applies to adults and not to children. We are, however, constantly changing our views and beliefs throughout our lifetime so the point at which one might call something transformative could be considered different for different people depending on their personal development. Whether younger people, say in their middle school or high school years, might have transformative learning experiences can be debated, but since those scholars who write about transformative learning are adult educators, most focus on learning that takes place in adulthood.

If a scholar primarily comes from a school of thought that views transformative learning as occurring through deeper changes to identity then the degree to which transformative learning can occur in younger years depends in good part on when identity is seen to be formed. From a cognitive perspective, at what stage of development can individuals engage in meta-cognition (thinking about their thinking)? From an intuitive, emotional, or relational perspective, do the developmental models limit shifts of habits of mind to a certain age or stage of development? This is less clear.

Jose describes his rough home life and his troubled relationships with his family in his younger years. The transformation he describes in this story began in a county jail years later. The story of Sung, as told by Nayoung, is about a person who is in the middle of a perspective transformation as a young adult (age 20). He may have started this re-orientation at the age of sixteen when he discovered the real reason his mother had abandoned him. Going back to Chapter 4, Art's story describes a very early decision to pursue a career choice as a result of an event he had experienced. That seems to us to be more a formative than a transformative experience. Knowles (1980) theory of andragogy was originally proposed as an adult learning theory, specifically as "the art and science of helping adults learn," but this perspective has been questioned. The extent to which transformative theory can be generalized to younger learners remains to be seen. In the meantime next are the stories of Jose and Sung to reflect upon.

THE GOOD ROAD – BY JOSE

As I write this, I am overwhelmed with feelings of euphoria as I am about six weeks away from receiving my master's degree. For some, this might be another goal to check off their list, but for me, it's all still a dream that I expect to wake up from. However, as I look back, my life wasn't always this great.

My name is Jose. I am a 38-year-old Hispanic male who was born right outside of San Francisco, California. I grew up in a ghetto located in the industrial city of South San Francisco. My parents who had emigrated from Mexico were very poor. As a result, I lived in a garage that was about 350 square-feet in area, which I shared with my parents and four siblings. Life in the box, which is what I called our home, was rough. My younger sister was born with a lung condition that required her to be confined to a crib wrapped with a plastic contraption and constant oxygen circulating to it. My father who was an alcoholic, and who was having an extramarital affair, spent his days at work and his nights and weekends away from home, either at the bar or with his mistress.

My sister's condition and my father's infidelity consumed my mother's attention. The majority of the time, my mother was very edgy. She would say some really mean things, and tell us to get out of the house. Since my house was one of two homes on the block, located in between a 76 gas station and a warehouse at the foot of a hill, there was not much to do. I would often go to a park located a couple of blocks away in a gang-infested neighborhood. The park was always littered with beer bottles, graffiti, and large groups of boys, but what drew my attention to this place was the unity and family-like relationships that the boys displayed, something that I yearned for. I would often stand close by and watch them hug, laugh, play, and joke around with each other, wishing that I could be part of the group. I had not experienced this sort of bond. The only thing that I was used to was being scolded at by my parents, which made me feel like I was the root of their problems.

The school that was closest to my house had closed down, so I was forced to go to the good school on the other side of town. Both of my parents only have a second grade education, so they were not able to provide me with educational support. As a result, school was very difficult for me. Everyone around me seemed so much smarter than I was, and this really made me feel incompetent and worthless. In addition, I was bullied a lot in school. I always tried to be transparent in the classroom, but the teacher would still call on me to answer. I always dreaded this not only because I did not know the answer, but because the students would almost always laugh at me. During recess, kids would mock me and call me stupid. There were even a few times when I was walking home that a couple of kids ran over to me and kicked me for no reason. I really hated going to school.

When I turned 12 years old, we moved to a one-bedroom house right in the heart of the ghetto, half a block from the park. Since I knew all of the boys, most of them gang-members, that hung around there, we quickly developed a family-like bond. Finally, I found the acceptance and protection that I had been missing in both my home and school life. Unfortunately, that bond also brought me many issues. That same year, I witnessed and often participated in constant violence. I even witnessed a stabbing and a shooting, which only intensified over the years. I also started experimenting with drugs. By the time I was 17, I had dropped out of school, was a full-fledged tattooed gang-member and a full-blown drug addict. My experiences, both as a gang-member and a drug addict, caused me a life of grief. I spent a total of 15 years in-and-out of jail, finally landing in San Quentin State Penitentiary.

Upon being released from prison, I tried to get my act together to impress my parole officer so that I could be released from parole sooner. I enrolled in a community college and pursued a certificate in dental assisting. I also obtained work, washing cars at a family-owned car rental agency, and I met my wife who later became my anchor. I did really well in school, which was a revelation. In addition, I was promoted at work to a rental agent position. My parole officer was really impressed, and, after 18 months, he terminated my parole. I kept a 4.0 GPA in my dental program and was a few months away from receiving my certificate, but when it was time to become certified, I did not pass the background check required. As a result, I did not receive a certificate. This was really difficult for me to swallow. Within months, I was also notified by my company that it was selling its business to the competition, and that I would no longer have a job.

I soon found myself in a state of depression. It wasn't long before my drug addiction resumed, and I began running the streets again. During this time, my wife was really supportive and she sat back waiting for me to snap out of it. She believed in me more than I believed in myself. My drug binge lasted for about 7 years before I landed in jail again. I was looking at a 12-year sentence. I bailed out of jail and enrolled in a drug rehabilitation program in an attempt to convince the judge to reduce my sentence. I didn't really care about what the drug rehabilitation program had to offer. My whole intention was to avoid going back to prison and to persuade the judge to give me another chance. I did an outstanding job at the drug program and even stayed there longer than I had to as a mentor to newcomers, but deep down inside nothing had changed. My strategy eventually worked. My outstanding performance convinced the judge, and he reduced my sentence to one year in the county jail, with the condition that I complete my time in the Choices program, a behavior modification program located within the county jail.

During this time, my wife waited patiently, visiting me every week without fail. She was very supportive and never once judged me. I don't recall much about the first four months of my stay in Choices, but the turning point for me was when I was sitting through one of the lectures. The lecture was about risk factors and how they impact our development and in the long run those we love. I clearly recall the lecturer, a visiting psychologist, say that we are not in control of what is done to us as children, but we are in control of the outcome. "So, you can choose to follow the bad road, or follow the good road," she said. At that moment, I had an epiphany. I was in control, and it was my choice to pick the good road or continue on a path of destruction. All I could think about was how selfish I had been. My wife had been very patient, hoping that I would turn my life around, and all I did was neglect her and our relationship. I could not fathom losing her. She was all that I had left. So from that point on, I decided that if I could not change for my own well-being, then I was going to do it for her.

When I was released from jail, I walked out with a goal and a new-found motivation. I immediately reported to my probation officer and explained that I was dedicated to turning my life around, but he just stared at me blankly. I am assuming that he had heard that many times before. He told me that, if I was serious, I should look into the county tattoo removal program. It wasn't long before I began the process of removing all of my tattoos, and in seven months, I was tattoo free. I also obtained temporary work through a staffing agency. I worked at a metal recycling company for about 90 days. Although they had offered me a job after the 90-day period, I did not accept it. I had saved enough money to buy a commercial van, so I went into business for myself, subcontracting deliveries and pickups for a freight forwarding company.

Shortly after, my wife and I bought our first home. Unfortunately, it was really close to where I grew up, and I often had people coming to look for me, unable to understand that I was no longer the same person. Since I was still on probation, and I did not want them to implicate me in any problems, I had to make another strategic decision. I knew that if I really wanted to be the person that I was meant to be, I was going to have to leave the environment in which I was raised. Consequently, my wife and I decided to sell the business and our home, and move to another state. My probation officer was really pleased with me. He supported my decision and granted me permission to leave the state of California and move to another state.

Once there, I knew that I would have to start all over. I obtained a temporary job working as a laborer for a construction company. Then, I found a job working as a laborer for a log home building company. I quickly excelled and became a supervisor. After about a year, the economic downturn took a toll on the housing market and I was laid off. I was forced to make a quick decision. So, I decided to give college another try. Fortunately, my wife was really supportive of my decision.

Shortly after, I enrolled in a community college and since I had dropped out of high school, I was forced to take remedial classes. There, I met a psychology professor who really inspired me to succeed. Her father had done research on juvenile delinquency and created a successful program in California based on his findings. She spent some time at that program and truly believed in giving people a second chance. As a result, she became my mentor and close friend. She helped me to believe in myself and to view my past as just that, my past. This allowed me to move forward vigorously, with a thirst for knowledge. It also motivated me to help at-risk populations.

After commencing school, I created a tutoring program between the college and a local school district to provide academic support to at-risk kids in poverty schools. I also developed many other programs such as a Thanksgiving program to help needy families during Thanksgiving, and a program to help elderly people with household chores and tasks. And, I spent my time volunteering for multiple programs and events such as the Family Literacy Program in which immigrant and refugee parents learn English while their children are cared for and tutored in different academic subjects.

While at community college, I also met a gentleman by the name of Peter who founded a program that helps juveniles and young adults disengage and exit gangs. Peter offered me an opportunity to join his organization as the tattoo removal program manager, a position that I accepted and currently hold today. This has allowed me to give back and help ex-gang members in so many ways. Being able to help and guide individuals out of a life of chaos and destruction, and become loving parents, husbands, and productive members of society has enriched my life. It also keeps me grounded and motivates me to want more out of life.

After taking all of my core classes at the community college, I decided to transfer to a local university, a decision that both my wife and mentor fully supported and encouraged. Two years later, I received my bachelor's degree in psychology. While there, I became a father of two healthy little boys. After graduating, I knew that I was not ready to stop learning, so I enrolled in a master's program at another university. This has been a great learning experience for me, and I can't wait to see what the future has in store. My journey is far from over. In fact, my journey has barely begun. I still have so much to learn and to contribute to this world. Nevertheless, I can confidently say that I am a good husband and a good role model to my children, and I can definitely provide them the structure, support, and direction that I so desperately needed as a child.

A STORY OF TRANSFORMATION OF A NORTH KOREAN STUDENT – BY NAYOUNG KIM

Freedom of education is nonexistent or a taboo in certain parts of the world. In such societies, the government injects propaganda and fear into school education to own the habits of mind of students at a young age. Students are deprived of freedom to learn, think, and reflect beyond the regime regulations. No questions asked, no answers given, but only information infused that will solidify people's loyalty to the regime. This is the life that many North Korean refugees share about their country. Unfortunately, their life in South Korea does not miraculously turn into a perfect dream as they have hoped. At the beginning phase of resettlement in South Korea, North Koreans are stunned by the amount of information bombarded on daily basis; a sudden shift from total deprivation to total freedom can be quite overbearing without sufficient support from the community. This can be especially challenging to North Korean adolescents and young adults in adapting to the rigorous education system in South Korea.

As an educator, it was both a challenging and rewarding experience to design curriculums for a camp that specifically aimed to excel 80 North Korean students as the next generation leaders in Korea. While developing materials for the camp, I consistently examined my assumptions about North Korean students and their education background. I realized that unchallenged assumptions can easily lead to another form of oppressive education system for these students. Though the camp was only for four days, many students shared testimonies on how the sessions helped them to revise their perspectives and develop greater self-awareness. The following testimony is from one participant in the camp who shares his life story and his dreams.

Sung (a pseudonym) is a 20 year old high school student who lived in an oppressive orientation for most of his life in North Korea. He recalls having few happy childhood memories. His family lived a meager lifestyle in the countryside. They were poor farmers but poverty did not stop them from sharing laughter and happiness. However, the severity of the harsh environment turned Sung's childhood and happiness into a nightmare. At the age of nine, he witnessed his father's death from severe hunger. Soon after, his mother vanished, abandoning her two children, and leaving them as orphans. She erased all traces of her existence in the family by destroying family photos and her personal belongings. This unexpected life crisis burdened the nine-year old Sung with new roles as a parent and provider for his younger sister. Also, Sung's orphan status downgraded his identity in society to 'mooyeongo,' which means "homeless and parentless." His surroundings were not sympathetic or understanding to his situation. He had no time to mourn or understand the sudden disruptions in his life. He had to swallow the harsh reality if he wanted to protect his and his younger sister's survival.

No one to trust. No one to depend on. No one to teach him tactics on how to survive. Day by day, he battled against hunger and poverty. Sung roamed around marketplaces, streets, and spent days at train stations where he might get lucky enough to find food crumbs. He begged. He stole. He lived this nomadic life for seven long years.

I was shocked to hear Sung's story, but more shocking was the calmness in his voice while sharing to fellow classmates during one of the mentoring sessions at the camp. This session encouraged students to reflect on their life journey and share on how it shaped their current sense of self. The age of these students ranges from 15 to 27 years old. They all attend an alternative school in South Korea that customizes its secondary education to North Korean students. Sung's classmates shared similar stories of a past that was filled with hunger, pain and death. They all defected to South Korea with a hope to live a dream life. However, this dream rapidly turned into pressure to fight for academic success. Sung continued his story.

One thing that kept Sung alive for seven years was his strong desire to reunite with his mother. Every day, he earnestly searched for reasons as to why his mother would disappear without any explanation. As time passed by, his feelings of betrayal and hatred grew stronger. He wanted to live. In fact, he had to live just to hear his mother's side of the story. At the age of 16, a miracle happened! His mother reached out to him for the first time and they reconnected over the phone. There was a flood of questions that he wanted to ask, but the conversation had to be kept short. One thing he found out was that his mother secretly escaped to China to earn money for the children's rescue. The conditions in North Korea were getting harsher, and she heard about job opportunities in China. The reason she erased all traces was to protect her children from the police who could potentially accuse the little ones as being a part of a traitor's family and send them to a prison camp. It is better to be thought of as dead than as a traitor of the regime. So, she felt it was safer to keep the truth away until she had enough resources to bring them out of the country. Sung was sixteen when he escaped to South Korea with the help of his mother. It had been four years since he came to South Korea, but he still could not reunite with her in person.

During the session, students openly shared their stories, both happy and dark moments in life. It was a powerful moment for each student who was sharing and hearing stories of courage, perseverance, and hope. For the first time, Sung became aware of a similar pattern of each story: moments of pain, obstacles, and moments of miracles. Before, all he could see were his own hardships in life, but the stories of classmates opened up a new level of confidence and self-esteem. He was not alone, and there was always a light at the end of the dark tunnel. He realized that he could determine his future by choosing to perceive challenges as meaningful opportunities. This self-actualization has led him to hold a different perspective about his dream to become a teacher. He was doubtful of his ability to achieve the dream because of the fierce competition to enter a national school of education. But now, Sung has gained the tools of confidence, skill building, and perspective taking so that he can take the next step in achieving his dream.

After the camp, Sung is now busy applying to universities to pursue his dream of becoming a teacher. It is still quite daunting to compete against the South Korean students and go through a rigorous interview process, but he feels different about himself. He mentions that he does not yet have all the clarity of his next steps, but he feels more competent than before. Lastly, his voice filled with great excitement as he talked about the last phone call he had with his mother. His mother is on her way to South Korea to reunite with Sung for the first time in 11 years. There is no more hatred and bitterness toward her; he only wishes to live as one family again.

COMMENTARY

Though formal education can be a vehicle for enlightenment, both Sung and Jose were causalities of an "oppressive education." Jose was forced to go to a "good school." His parents were unable to provide support, and school was very difficult for him. The other students were "smart" and Jose felt incompetent. He was bullied, the students laughed at him, and he dreaded the teacher calling on him to answer questions. Those around him, teacher and students, limited his ability to succeed and to reach his full potential. It makes one cringe to hear him describe his humiliation and feelings of worthlessness. This is how the educational system can contribute to the development of distorted meaning perspectives. The story describes how his mentor, a community college psychology instructor, was able to help him to reconsider the limiting assumptions he experienced in school. This is how the educational system, this time in the form of a teacher, can help people question and revise their assumptions to reflect potential and hope.

Jose's assumptions about his ability to learn were formed in childhood. Naturally enough, it took considerable time for him to revise the way he saw himself. Before he could engage in this journey, he became a gang member and an addict, activities that led him to prison. He spent 15 years in and out of prison. He was finally able to enter into the educational system, but he failed a background check, and was plunged into depression, drug use, and more jail time. He encountered his first turning point in a rehabilitation program in jail when he was listening to a lecture by a visiting psychologist. From there, it was still a few more steps before he found a supportive educational environment and a teacher/mentor. At this point, he was able to transform his perspectives and assumptions related to his ability to learn.

Sung's story is told by Nayoung, who worked with him in her role as director of curriculum and content development for an educational organization in South Korea which works with students formerly from North Korea who have lived in extremely difficult circumstances. Here we see the generative possibilities of educational programs and how they can facilitate changes in worldview and personal identity. Sung's early childhood was filled with loss and feelings of abandonment and deprivation, and at the age of nine he was without both parents. He survived driven by the need to find out why his mother had abandoned him and by the desire to reunite with her. The reader does not know for sure the assumptions that drove Sung's behavior and his feelings of betrayal and hurt toward his mother, but it is likely that he assumed his mother did not love him and had left him for an easier life. That assumption was at least challenged—we aren't sure if he really felt loved immediately or how much that assumption really changed—when he met his mother at the age of 16. At that young age he began a transformation toward a more open and better justified perspective that was reinforced by the opportunities to reflect and to be a part of the loving and supporting learning environment that was provided by Nayoung's program. Still just 20, his perspective continued to become more open to the possibilities of the world as his beliefs in his own value grew through the care shown him by volunteers in the program, and also by the relationship that he continued to rebuild with his mother.

The stories of both Jose and Sung illustrate the power of a positive educational experience and the roles of helpful, caring educators who continued to believe in them in spite of the obstacles they faced. For both of these young men, relationships with educators fostered transformative learning; this happened sooner for Sung and later for Jose, but the processes were parallel in form and content.

TRANSFORMATIVE LEARNING AND SOCIAL CHANGE

The power of the Highlander experience is the strength that grows within the souls of people, working together, as they analyze and confirm their own experiences and draw upon their understanding to contribute to fundamental change. (from Highlander's 1987 Mission Statement)

John M. Glen, *Highlander: No Ordinary School*, 1996, p. 286

Historically, adult education focused on social change. The earliest descriptions of adult education were related to efforts to increase literacy among adults in Great Britain (Selman, 1989); in the 1700's the work of these educators was seen to be politically motivated and dangerous to the status quo in that people who learned to read and write would become informed and able to critique the existing social state. In the early 1900s, the Antigonish Movement in Canada and the Highlander Folk School in the United States were focused not only on literacy but on helping workers develop economic independence and freedom from oppression. With the exception of Freire's (1970) work with adult literacy in South America, the goal of social change was almost lost when humanism became the pervasive philosophical foundation of adult education (Knowles, 1975, 1980). Mezirow's (1991) theory of transformative learning fell into a humanist, constructivist, and individually oriented category, and it was criticized for its neglect of social change.

Today, researchers and writers still tend to emphasize individuals' transformative learning, but there is more awareness of how it includes the promotion of social change and more frequent calls to consider how transformative learning theory can address issues related to political and social oppression.

In this chapter, we illustrate transformative learning as social change with two quite different stories. Olutoyin lives and works in Nigeria. She has dedicated her work as an adult educator to helping women in Nigeria to become free from oppression. Her book, *Women and Power: Education, Religion, and Identity* (2012) chronicles the stories of those women and her founding of WARSHE (Women against Rape, Sexual Harassment, and Sexual Exploitation) and presents a powerful and deeply disturbing study of Nigerian women and advocacy for Nigerian women.

Mike Kim offers the second story in this chapter. Mike describes himself as an Asian Latino American Veteran; he is a veteran of the war in Iraq who has readjustment issues from the Iraq war. He is currently working to understand his experience through his doctoral studies, and also his work with other veterans. He recognizes the necessity of social change in response to war experiences. Mike leads workshop groups, reaches out to other veterans, speaks at conferences, and dedicates himself to social change for veterans.

MY STORY – BY OLUTOYIN MEJIUNI, DEPARTMENT OF CONTINUING EDUCATION, OBAFEMI AWOLOWO UNIVERSITY ILE-IFE, NIGERIA

When a mother of five, who had only primary school education, was summoned by a customary court, she did not know what was going to befall her. Apparently, her husband had asked the court to dissolve the marriage they contracted by native law and custom. The court dissolved her marriage of about 15 years and awarded custody of all the children, including the one that was less than eight years old to her husband, who had no clear source of livelihood. He sent her packing, and she was distressed, but she reported at her work in a formal setting every day and took food and other provisions to her children in their father's house once a week. About four months after the dissolution of her marriage, she appeared at the WARSHE (Women against Rape, Sexual Harassment and Exploitation) office. Her boss told her to go and seek support from WARSHE, because two days earlier, her husband who had been stalking her, met her at a bus stop, pursued her into the bus she wanted to board, dragged her down, punched and beat her up, and dragged her on the floor while she struggled to free herself. When persons at the bus stop made to stop him, he said the woman was his wife, who ran away from home. This woman set herself free and rushed inside the bus. Her ex-husband pursued the bus, double crossed the bus and was going to grab and begin to beat his ex-wife again, when the high school students who were around prepared to pounce on him. He fled.

When this woman appeared in the WARSHE office, she was in a bad shape. She said her ex-husband, who married her while she was a teenager to the dismay of her parents, and who did not allow her to further her education, resented the fact that she had a regular job, and had promised to trash her at her workplace so she would be fired. He was demanding money for his upkeep, and was alleging that she was going out with other men. He had even gone on to threaten two of the men he had seen with her, promising he would send them six feet below. We urged her to lodge a complaint with the police. She was reluctant because she had been there, and the issue was treated as a 'family matter'. She had also been to the social welfare department, and the officers there urged her to pray so he would change. We supported her to lodge a complaint with the police. This had no effect as he kept stalking and threatening her. So WARSHE wrote the head of the police, asking him to restrain our client's ex-husband from causing her harm. The police dithered and then summoned a meeting of our client, her ex-husband, and WARSHE volunteers. Our client's ex-husband did not show up, so the head of the police ordered his men to bring him to the station. When he was asked about his relationship with our client, he declared that she was his wife. The head of police asked: "you mean ex-wife?"

He said "no, she is my wife." The police official who had seen the divorce papers from the customary court was stunned, so were we four WARSHE volunteers who were at the meeting. The police asked our client to formally show evidence that they were divorced. The woman produced the divorce papers, and the police officer asked the man why he was claiming that the woman was his wife after he had filed for divorce and his wishes had been granted, and he had sent her packing with plenty of violence. He kept insisting that our client was his wife. When the policeman asked the woman to state her demands, she made the point that she wanted the police to tell her ex-husband to leave her to enjoy her peace. As she narrated how he had abused her over the years, and how he charged at her like a bulldog, the police ordered that he be locked up and charged in court the following morning.

When our client and WARSHE staff reported at the court house the following morning, neither our client's ex-husband nor the police were there. When they went to the police station, there were pleas that the man would turn a new leaf and let our client be. He left her alone for about three months and resumed harassment of all men that she interacted with. With the support of WARSHE staff, she went back to the police, who told our client's ex-husband that they had it, he would either stay away from her or they would get him to face the law. A year after this WARSHE client first came into our office, I arrived at the WARSHE office for a meeting. I noticed that the WARSHE intervention officer had just seen a woman off, so I packed my car, and had walked past the woman when the WARSHE intervention officer called her back into the office and introduced her to me. Apparently, the WARSHE staff noticed neither of us recognized the other. I was pleasantly shocked. In front of me was an absolutely beautiful woman, who was neatly and smartly dressed, and who looked radiant and confident.

As a part of my own transformation from a politically aware person, union activist and humanist to a feminist in 1997, I and two colleagues decided to create an organizational structure unencumbered by deeply held convictions and/or prejudices that: consider victims as deserving of their ordeals; consider certain matters unworthy or too private to be pursued; or consider that certain matters are "normal" male-female interactions. We were motivated by two horrible cases of rape and gang rape that were reported to my colleague and me, and the whispers of, and media reportage of sexual violence against women in the private and the public spheres. In this way, WARSHE—Women against Rape, Sexual Harassment and Sexual Exploitation—was launched with a three-day intensive training workshop for the core volunteers: university teachers, professionals and university students. From the beginning, we defined the organization as a feminist organization that was out to improve the social status of Nigerian women, through prevention and protection against sexual violence and abuse (SVA), and helping women and children cope when abuses occur. WARSHE turned 15 in October 2013, and in 15 years, there were 153 major and mini educational programs implemented and managed, comprising intensive training workshops; symposia; and awareness raising and sensitization talks and exercises. WARSHE also received and documented reports of 71 cases of sexual violence and abuse and other forms of gender-based violence in the office at Ile-Ife, Nigeria and supported victims and survivors.

It is in this context that I have witnessed and supported many transformative learning stories, one of which I described in the opening of this writing. Another story took place two hours into a symposium held for high school students in a town hall in a major city in Southwest Nigeria, we (the WARSHE volunteers who served as resource persons at the symposium) told the high school students that it was time for questions, answers and comments. For two hours before the question period four of us had taken turns to define and describe different forms of sexual violence and abuse, where they occur, the perpetrators, the repercussions, and why women are usually the victims and potential victims. We also described self-defense and coping strategies. In the middle of the session, a middle aged man, apparently one of the workers in the town hall, walked to the stage where we, the resource persons, were seated, from the back stage, and signaled, as he also declared by word of mouth, in the Yoruba language (the language of the people of Southwest Nigeria) that he wanted to ask a question. We gave him the microphone and he said: "I have been listening to you, and I got the impression that you are saying a man can rape his wife." The resource person who was most skilled in the Yoruba language responded, with a clear explanation of what constituted consensual sex, and what constituted rape. When she was done, the town hall worker who had listened to her with rapt attention said: "I promise you, as from today onwards, it will never happen again." All of us in the hall broke out in loud applause. We did not ask him for the details of what he had been doing. That solemn promise, made without coercion, was what we needed. On my own part, the applause was to encourage him to go and do as he has promised.

The reaction of this man was not atypical during and after the WARSHE education programs. Professionals who were participants in the WARSHE programs have broken their silence on the abuses they had suffered or that loved ones had suffered; a few male participants have openly identified themselves as "feminists"; while some of the medical doctors and police officers who have attended WARSHE workshops have alerted WARSHE to cases of rape that had been presented by victims in their clinics and stations, and that were either going to be mishandled by medical personnel and the police, or that they thought would benefit from WARSHE intervention. In one instance, the doctor did not just alert WARSHE, she played an activist role, linking up with the police, and putting in extra efforts to ensure that the medical tests required in a case of rape were carried out in hospitals that had better facilities than the one she worked for. She announced that she was a WARSHE volunteer to whoever cared to listen, and much later, shared the story of how she had to abandon one medical school for another, because of sexual harassment.

About nine years ago, during the 16 days of activism campaign against gender-based violence, wearing T-shirts with messages that discourage gender-based violence; and armed with stickers, fliers, and posters, WARSHE volunteers, led by members of the Coordinating Council of WARSHE, embarked on campaigns on campuses of five higher institutions and their host communities in five towns in Southwest Nigeria. The volunteers consisted mainly of students and a few lecturers. Each campaign team went round their campus, talking to persons whom they met and handing out sensitization materials. We visited female hostels where the institution were residential; and then moved to town, specifically to police stations, court and media houses, and the Departments of Education and Social Welfare. The campaign was a sensitization and advocacy exercise; and also a kind of subtle and overt pressure on all to desist from abusing women, and not to condone the abuse of women.

The campaign afforded us, the Coordinating Council of WARSHE (who are also university lecturers) the opportunity to discover assets and talents among the students in the campaign teams. Some were direct and hard campaigners, while some were subtle and persistent, such that they got persons who were totally uninterested in the subject of violence against women to listen to them. In addition, the mostly positive, and the few extremely negative reactions and responses of persons that the teams met during the campaigns generated passionate discussions, and direct and indirect witnessing to instances of violence against women among the students, mainly inside the vehicles that conveyed us to and from some of the settings we had targeted for the campaign. It is possible that we assume that the students are converts, and so their reactions were to be expected. Even then, it is good to know that critical self reflection and the validation of experiences go on among those who take on the task of stimulating the process of helping others to engage in critical reflection on experiences.

I know that there is much work to be done in changing the social status of Nigerian women and reducing the incidence of sexual violence abuse; and that worries me. However, I have found peace in knowing that I participated in building an organization that has the character to continue to insist on respect and dignity for women and children.

MY STORY – BY MIKE KIM, COLUMBIA UNIVERSITY DOCTORAL STUDENT, IRAQ WAR VETERAN, AND PSYCHOANALYST

"Where did that get you?" were her words to me as I mentioned my desire to return to the military. This was my then girlfriend scolding me shortly after my return from Iraq. These words rattled me for I did not think my desire to serve in the military again for a fourth time deserved a scolding. This was part of the collection of "Welcome Home" happenings after my return from Iraq.

Frankly, I really didn't want a hero's welcome. I was not looking for a parade! What else didn't I want? Not the free polyester "veterans, we care" backpack (showing off a veteran interest group), nor did I want the 10% veteran discounts on overpriced chainsaws and patio chairs.

What did I want? Maybe, seeing America truly communalize 12 years of war could have alleviated some of my frustrations. Veterans should not be generalized objects of interest; they should not be prey for politicians, profiteers and opportunists. Maybe, seeing the resentment from many non-post 9/11 veterans subside would inspire more dialogue? Many veterans think Iraq /Afghanistan veterans get all the attention from American society. But, is it a constructive attention or more of way of sensationalizing these war years instead of accurately assessing the damages from being in a constant state of war?

Prior to Iraq, I was intact and left my home intact. That is right, my life was left clean before I left for Iraq, especially, so, in case I returned to America as a dead man, the preachers and sinners would've still said, "Mike Kim was a good man!" at the veteran's cemetery. I survived Iraq and my life was not the same when I returned. I placed certain priorities aside such as a private professional practice, a doctoral degree program and other important things. So, what did I really want? Something more than this image: I remember the rainy cold night five years ago; I was in combat fatigues at Newark Airport. There were no familiar faces around; I was alone.

The barrage of overwhelming post-war reintegration encounters were like enemy rockets hitting my assumptions of "Home." I was left with piercing questions about "Home." Why has the veteran community not promoted diverse voices regarding the reintegration process? Instead, the war documentaries such as *Restrepo* are telling the stories of veterans. Why aren't the veterans telling the stories? These movies tend to retrigger the warriors and create hordes of war voyeurs in TV/movie land. The documentarians and the veteran lobby groups carry the veteran voice. Why are some clinicians, researchers, politicians, journalists, filmmakers and others flocking to engage veterans without hearing the voices of the veterans they are engaging? I am not interested in the long sad gazes into the veteran world. Is there a way to reflect, understand and act in the context of healing from war?

Some attractive researcher showed up to a veteran student group I was facilitating at a CUNY College. She was recruiting veterans for a research study that had little relevance to the veterans present: psycho-biological challenges, existential inquiries, ecological spaces, human traverses, and potential joys/dreams of veterans were not engaged by the study. What is the purpose of gazing into the lives of many pained veterans? Why wasn't the study trying to capture the lived experience of the veteran?

At a huge Manhattan Church, there was a veteran civilian dialogue project that basically paraded the pain of veterans without providing anything to improve the lives of those on parade. Can a veteran's voice be heard? Can authentic relationships be developed to better understand the acute issues with combat trauma survivors?

At several highly publicized writing veteran workshops, I found myself as a subaltern without a voice. Was it that I am an Asian Latino American Veteran? The invisible Asian American veteran is rarely seen in Yellow Ribbon "Welcome Home" fever. Was it my educational background? What was it? E.L. Doctorow, the author of the great American novel *Ragtime*, attended a veteran writing workshop and could not understand why I needed to write war fiction in a style that was fragmented and postmodern. He wanted me to look at Hemingway and others from the traditional military literature canon. He never asked me about my style? He did not know that I wanted the disorder of war to be central in my writings.

My resistance towards Doctorow came down to this: What did Hemingway offer me regarding my less than masculine sentiments of a dying Iraqi girl? General George S. Patton's hypermasculine reflections of war *War as I Knew It*, but I wonder the reactions if Patton wrote a book titled "War as I Felt It." This type of war literature did not draw me into the multiplicity of stories that war offers from diverse troops.

It was probably hard for E.L. Doctorow to absorb my tangential writing loaded with references from disparate realities and emotions and not hero worship:

> Before Iraq, Monty was known as "Miguel Montgomery Kim." He once carried the incredible: a Yale Mory's Cup shine and the pride of Asia and Las AMericas in his face. This he did not have for the old shepherd on the road. The moment shared with the old man blunted Monty's flow along the Spanish road into clouds of dissociation. Who knows what the old man said to trigger Monty?
>
> Even Quixote never experienced such a haze in his bout with the windmills. Such a sad lost feeling. Monty had been taken farther from himself in the exchange with the old man. The psychic dragons had blown their fire on Monty. Did Quixote ever have to deal with troubles on his trot on a Spanish road? Did Quixote in all of his courage to dream and will have to deal with a woman offering to hand over her dead child?" (from the ending to a postmodern war story "Oye Loco" by Mike Kim)

In my writing, there was something disorienting for Doctorow and I; while I found this chaos of words healing to write, I felt that others and I needed to pursue critical reflections towards the war literature canon. I did not find value in suppressing my fragmented writing style. After the Doctorow experience, I broke from the less than freeing veteran writing projects and created an open veteran narrative writing group (featured on APM public radio's "War and Words"). This group sparked vet writers to create other narrative writing groups in the City. These groups did not have an MFA instructor directing the writing styles of vet writers; they used writing as a way to engage feelings and thoughts about war. There was not a politicized agenda with these groups.

After several disappointments seeking ways to have dialogue with civilians about veteran readjustment, I was led to General Semantics by a Canadian civilian classmate from my doctoral program at Columbia, Blake Seidenshaw. This led me to an authentic conversation about veteran readjustment with Dr. Martin Levinson, President of the Institute of General Semantics. Levinson and I have looked at readjustment myths of previous wars to find ways to engage the present veteran readjustment approaches for veterans and those working with veterans. Our dialogue has led us to look at Alfred Korzybski, founder of General Semantics, who promoted a trailblazing adult learning mental "bootcamp" for troops. It was successfully implemented by U.S Army psychologist LTC Douglas M. Kelley for combat soldiers fighting in Europe during WW II. By the way, General Semantics has influenced the clinical work of some credible practitioners: Albert Ellis, Fritz Perls, William Alanson White, S.I. Hiyakawa, and others. The dialogue with Levinson has helped me to be like the civilian I used to be prior to going to war. We have discussed many aspects of readjustment; He has empowered me with guidance in work with veterans using the General Semantics method for constructively reframing thoughts related to war.

My war torn family, my former life as a contemplative friar, and my job as a combat trauma readjustment counselor have provided meanings in my life that help me deal with my present life.

My parents, my only sibling and I have deeply experienced war. The war experience has clouded us, but has also oriented us. Not too many American families have this in their home. We were not the Waltons!

My sister was deployed to Afghanistan with the U.S. Army. She returned from war and we are "battle buddies" in the reintegration process. We talk every day. Unconsciously, I know we mention things about our war experience, frequently. We help each other! We look at solutions to problems and resolve them.

My mother told me many times about jets bombing areas near her lovely home. She would hide under the bed and patiently wait for the attacks to end. Ironically, most people ask "did you ever kill anybody?" but they never ask, "were you ever unsafe?" My mother's war experience inspired me to look at safety as more of an issue of self care and not something to ignore while in a war.

My mother would say, "....character is found in the man wearing the uniform." Famed Vietnam War author Tim O'Brien writes that a true war story does not moralize. But, my mother is a reminder that morality must not be lost in war, and must have a place in the true war story.

My father, for all of his coldness, I accept him. Where does the coldness come from? Was the Japanese occupation of Korea an enslaving experience? He experienced the Inchon landing as a displaced person during the Korean War? He ran patrols with the Korean 5th Infantry Division? I know few things about my father. Yet, I know that his life has involved an ugliness that also embraces healing vulnerable animals; he was a public health veterinarian for most of his adult life. He also remained married to my mother until she died of cancer. Maybe, my father inspired me to create a warzone project "Team Rawan" for Iraqi children. The vulnerable child was sent to India for medical care and seen by one of Mother Teresa's former doctors.

My family experienced war and knowing that they carry pain but also carry compassion has helped me to imagine a future that is not completely damned. My future does not have to be a tragic or triumphant spectacle featured in the NY Times War Blog. Understanding my family's journey in war has freed me from the myths of home often paraded in the Sunday paper or on film.

My vowed priory (monastery) experience gave me a gift for the rest of my life. I rejoined the military after spending 10 years on a spiritual journey going back to

Yale Divinity School and then selling my Ford truck to the local Catholic Worker House for a discernment pilgrimage in Spain. I walked 300 miles in thirty days the Camino de Santiago to discern my calling as Dominican Friar. The Dominicans taught me that spirituality involved not just reflecting. From one of my veteran narrative groups a poem blossomed showing the complexity yet union of the rifle and the robe:

(a Korean Sijo poem named "monk at war" by mike kim) "Alone, one hot day, a boy, in full flight carries a brown package this Iraqi boy runs to me and my trigger finger tempts me. Beyond bravado I contemplate psalms 23 and let boy pass."

An uncommon life of monastery to war unfolded for me. I moved from a prayer stall to the seat of a Humvee combat vehicle. And yet, after I left my vows to rejoin the military, I recognized that my life changed and I became a shaman. Though, I was a regular combat troop, I was open to the stories of other troops and provided guidance. I was a licensed psychoanalyst and this was invaluable. Though I was a soldier, and I was not in the medical corps, informally, I had been a witness to the complex accounts of war and home for many. In a deep transpersonal way, I already knew about many intimate things that would unfold for my fellow troops. I would mediate between the important realms of war and home and provide guidance. The shaman of my ancestry probes problems and is a humble guide and helps the wounded soul discern. This is healing. The shaman is like the ferryman in the Epic of Gilgamesh. I was also a shaman to several Iraqis and felt obligated to provide compassion and guidance to them.

I want to keep discerning my life and I want to keep helping others discern war. I also want those devastated by war to not only deconstruct myths; but to discern the myths of war. How is war situated in the life that is lived? This is something I learn every day, in my job, at the Vet Center. The staff and the veterans who come to heal teach me many things to keep my shamanic presence for those who are still trying to find home.

Now, I can tell the woman who left me after my return from Iraq a few more things about her scolding, "Where did that get you?"

COMMENTARY

When we first put these two stories together, we were hesitant about how well they both worked to illustrate transformative learning as social change. But when the stories were placed one after the other, the parallels stood out—different countries, different circumstances, but two educators working to create social change in their context. Olutoyin's story describes her own transformation as she comes to understand herself as moving from a politically aware person, union activist and humanist to a feminist in 1997. As a result of this transformation, she and two colleagues decided to create an organizational structure for supporting and promoting change among women in Nigeria. Olutoyin's story clearly illustrates her efforts to promote social change through WARSHE; her story also introduces us to the powerful stories of the people who have come to WARSHE for help—an abused women who came to WARSHE, and a man who came to understand the meaning of "rape." Her story has at least two layers—her own story of founding WARSHE and the stories of the people who were helped by WARSHE. In these layers, we see the layers of transformative learning that include individual stories and stories of social change. Both can and do exist simultaneously.

Mike's story contains the same layers. It is both a story of his experience as an Iraqi veteran who is experiencing challenges after the war and post-war reintegration issues, and a story of how he is working to help other veterans through the same experience. He describes his return from his time in Iraq and the difficulties he experienced with the way he was greeted by others. Mike also goes on to describe how he has ventured into the world of helping others who share his experience. He has sponsored dialogue groups, writing groups, and a "boot camp" for veterans. But at the same time he writes, "I am not interested in the long sad gazes into the veteran world." He does not want to be pitied or studied or misunderstood by those individuals who have not shared his experience, but as an adult educator, he works toward social change in much the same way as Olutoyin does.

CHAPTER 8

TRANSFORMATIVE LEARNING AND SPIRITUALITY

People say that what we're all seeking is a meaning for life. I don't think that's what we're really seeking. I think that what we're seeking is an experience of being alive, so that our life experiences on the purely physical plane will have resonances within our innermost being and reality, so that we actually feel the rapture of being alive.

Joseph Campbell, *The Power of Myth*, 1988, pp. 4–5

According to Thomas Moore in *Care of the Soul*, "'Soul' is not a thing, but is rather a quality or a dimension of experiencing life and ourselves. It has to do with depth, value, relatedness, and personal substance" (1992, p. 5). Caring for the soul, he says, is not primarily about problem solving but more about giving "ordinary life the depth and value that come with soulfulness" (p. 4). Both Kelly and Libby in this chapter seem to be seeking to observe and to understand their soul in this sense, and they both use walking to develop the stories of their transformative journeys. Kelly tells us about a hike along the trail with her dog Tanner, Libby about her 500-mile pilgrimage along the route of the Camino de Santiago. Kelly uses her walk as a metaphor, to help explain how she has moved forward and the twists and turns and ups and downs along the way. Libby's hike more directly contributes to her transformation, and she describes what she has learned from her pilgrimage.

Taking a journey has long been used as a metaphor for understanding our lives. The *Divine Comedy* (2003), possibly the greatest poem ever written and one of the world's great pieces of literature, is the story of Dante's trip, guided by his mentor Virgil, through the depths of hell, on to purgatory, and then to heaven. Robert Frost's (1946) poem, "The Road Not Taken", finds a traveler with a dilemma. Presented with two paths, shall the sojourner take the one which most had chosen, or the other? The choice was, as Frost writes, "I took the one less traveled by/And that has made all the difference" (p. 117). David Whyte (1994) describes work as a pilgrimage. Looking at it that way, he says, "is to put our heart's desires to hazard, because by merely setting out, we have told ourselves that there is something bigger and better, or even smaller and better – above all, something more life giving – that awaits us in our work and we are going to seek it" (p. 13).

Charaniya (2012) uses the phrase "journey of transformation" (p. 231) to describe a repeating three-part sequence in the transformative learning process, looked at in a spirituality or cultural context. She sees transformation from this perspective as something that changes how a person defines her or his place in the world.

Spirituality, say Tolliver and Tisdell (2006), "is about meaning making and a sense of wholeness, healing, and the interconnectedness of all things. Spirituality is different than religion: it is about an individual's journey toward wholeness..." (p. 38). O'Sullivan (2012) uses almost the same words to describe transformative learning. Tolliver and Tisdell think that learning, which "permeates one's whole self, [and] which has a spiritual component" (p. 38), has a higher probability of being transformative than that which is limited to the rational critical reflection of assumptions. Since spirituality involves meaning making then transformation of meaning schemes can be spiritually connected. This is not unimportant to adults, many of whom find spirituality to be a meaningful part of their lives. Both Kelly and Libby describe journeys taken which are spiritual in the sense of looking for meaning.

FREEING THE KIMONO – BY KELLY ANDERSON

The trail is empty of the usual runners and mountain bikers today. The bitter wind must have kept them indoors. But for me, the splendid blue sky and warm sunshine make the battle worth it. The view across the city below, dressed in its brilliant fall color, is breathtaking. And the open mountain ranges on the far side of the valley are inspiring.

Tanner and I will enjoy a couple of hours of complete solitude. Even he seems to feel the peace and only occasionally strains at his leash. The open space and fresh, brittle air has cleared the way for deep thoughts and I try to focus my thinking on the future. I have some decisions to make and need to find some clarity. This kind of day is often what I need to open up and let my dreams take form. But right now, my thoughts will not be focused. My mind is set on wandering. It is the past that draws my attention.

I'm thinking of the reflective piece that I wrote about a year ago. I loved the words that emerged that day and the story is worth repeating.

When I initially freed the kimono, I didn't really see it as exactly that. I just wanted to take it out of the glass box that enclosed it for almost twenty years. It was later that I started to think of it in a symbolic way, as a metaphor for my transformation and growth.

The kimono came to me as a gift from Dad. He brought it home from Tokyo after another long business trip. It was lovely, silk, and Japanese—all very appealing to a little girl. I was enchanted and couldn't wait to show it to my friends.

My parents reluctantly allowed me to wear it to school for show-and-tell, with the caution that I was to take care and not let it get dirty. I was seven years old and, although I tried very hard to keep the hem lifted, I sometimes forgot, allowing it to trail behind, dragging on the ground. By the end of the day, the bottom was grimy. The kimono was taken away from me and I didn't see it for another twenty years.

It was after I was married and my husband and I had built our new home that the kimono reappeared. My parents framed it in a huge glass shadow box and brought it to me as a house-warming gift. The kimono was carefully arranged in a T shape to properly display the beautiful lines and draping sleeves. It was fastened firmly to the stiffened linen backing with clear fishing line. And it had been cleaned to eliminate all traces of the dirt along the hem. I hung it in a prominent place.

Another twenty years passed and I found myself wanting to remove the kimono from the box. I had a vision for it. I commissioned a local artist to create a metal form in the shape of a dancing woman that I could dress in the robe. She did a wonderful job of bringing my vision to life. Now I love the kimono as much as I did when Dad gave it to me those many years ago. I named her Bella.

It was some time after I'd freed the kimono from the box that I started appreciating its symbolism. Initially it had been tightly controlled. Then it was brought out, but protected and contained. It was anchored by invisible strings and displayed in a rigid frame to show off its best features. Now it's out of the box and able to breathe.

Bella is a daily reminder to me. To be on a transformative journey you must be willing to change your frame of reference and break loose of the hidden strings that tie you to your old beliefs and assumptions. The process of change comes with the risk that you won't always display only your best features, you might get messy and expose some flaws, but it offers the potential of finding a beautiful flow.

As Tanner and I climb the steep southwest side of the Polecat Loop Trail, I reflect on that story. The kimono truly is symbolic of how I feel. But, it's only a part of the story. The circumstances that initiated the changes in my life, and the conditions that facilitated and encouraged those changes, should be explored. And the tangible differences in my life that followed the new awareness and freedom are also important to the story.

It's difficult to say exactly what started me on my journey. Normal growth and maturity are undoubtedly a part of it. Many people re-evaluate their life as they approach fifty. For me, that time coincided with another difficult change. My only child decided to go to college on the other side of the country. He was my world and his departure left me empty and, quite literally, experiencing genuine feelings of grief.

All of that was certainly a catalyst for change, however many people experience difficult times, even traumatic and permanent losses, and eventually return to their normal life. This wasn't true for me.

I simply did not want to fill that space with whatever little things crept in. I wanted to bring something new and significant into my life. And I wanted to be intentional about it. But I had no idea what I really wanted to do and I needed a space for self-exploration. The options for achieving that were countless. I could have taken up Yoga, or fly-fishing, or knitting, or any other hobby. Luckily, I chose to go back to college.

I took a rational approach and searched my options for something that would enhance my career. I narrowed down the field to a couple of good possibilities. Then I chose a program that wasn't even on my list and met none of the criteria I had established. Yeah me!

During the previous year I had attended a brown bag lunch event at a local college campus where a professor presented on the topic of work and finding your passion.

The lecture came out of a program in the university's Department of Education. As an accountant, I'd always focused my education on business and had never considered participating in any other type of program. But I kept finding myself thinking about the luncheon discussion and eventually followed my heart and applied for admission to that program. It was the right move.

The program covered a broad range of subjects. The courses were diverse, from very theoretical explorations of leadership and organizational development, to very practical skills based work in such things as instructional design, program planning and career development. Centered at the heart of it all was adult learning.

Predominately web-based, the courses involved a significant amount of reading, reflective writing and online dialogue. Sharing our individual life experiences was encouraged and an environment of open acceptance was cultivated. This was just what I was searching for and I loved every minute of it. In hindsight, I now know that this was also a prescription for transformation.

Just like the hiking terrain that we've just passed through, the coursework led me through highs and lows, with expansive views appearing briefly only to disappear with the next turn of the trail. The north face of Polecat is rugged and the switchbacks keep the path ahead mostly hidden, but the promise of wonderful surprises, combined with the occasional glimpse of the landscape ahead encouraged me forward.

It wasn't, however, the program alone that led to the changes that I now feel. Assignments and study materials often piqued my interest and led to new discoveries. One assignment that required participation in a new learning experience led me to train as a tutor and start volunteering with adult learners. Four years later I still spend one evening each week tutoring adult GED students. It's the best part of my week. Another assignment that required attendance at a meeting of a human resource related organization led me to join the ASTD. Through that organization I've attended some very motivational events.

A few pivotal moments from the past few years that would seem to be completely unrelated to my formal education also stand out. I can still hear the words of Sal Khan of the Khan Academy when he suggested that he didn't want his acceptance into an elite college to be his greatest achievement. And my own thought in response to that – I probably didn't want *my son's* acceptance into an elite college to be the greatest achievement of my life. Good point, Sal.

And I remember vividly a couple of Rice University lectures I attended while visiting my son at school. Dr. Malcolm Gillis' discussion of economic development through bottom up change has greatly influenced my thinking. And Dr. Richard Baraniuk set my course with his presentation on the importance of Networks of Knowledge and technology as a key enabler for that. While these lectures weren't connected to any of my academic classes, it was probably my work in the program that had shifted my perspective and allowed me to hear and be moved by the messages.

I can't define exactly when, but somewhere along the way these new activities became the norm for me. My interests are different now. I spend my free time working with those who have greater challenges than I can even begin to imagine. I believe passionately in the power of education to improve lives. I am excited about the unimaginable potential of technology and open-source learning tools to radically change the world. I feel a personal responsibility to use my gifts to help those who were not as fortunate as me. As someone who was lucky enough to be born with capabilities and resources in a time and place that allows me to develop those advantages, I want to use them for good. And I find it increasingly difficult to spend my workday in the same way that I have for all of my professional life.

My previous focus was much like that of my friends, family and colleagues. The priority was to build a comfortable life and try to do good along the way. However, to be quite honest, my definition of a "comfortable life" was slowly moving towards a life of luxury and excess. I no longer find pleasure in that.

I'm a practical person. It's been difficult to leave a safe career and good job with many benefits. So while my thoughts and free time are spent in ways that are dramatically different than in the past, I've haven't been able to make the very scary decision to dramatically change my career and my life. But I'm approaching the point where maintaining the status quo simply won't be an option for me, no matter what the price of change.

We've now rounded the northeastern bend of the loop and reached a high point on our hiking trail. Below me I can see the path stretching forward, through the gentle, rolling meadow of the Polecat Gulch. The path is fully visible and it will eventually bring us full circle to our destination. That final point on today's trek is still hidden, there's one more sharp turn. And this is very much where I am on my personal journal of transformation too. I don't know precisely what my future looks like. But the path is very clear now.

I'm now working towards a second Masters degree. With its focus on the hard skills utilized in educational technology, it's an entirely different type of program than the one that led to the changes I've experienced. The work is very technical, but it will help me develop the very specific skills that I need to contribute in the meaningful way that I want to. I'm learning to build the platform from which to project the voice that I've found.

The downward sloping meadow and the wind now at my back encourage me to pick up the pace. And I focus my thoughts to what's ahead in my life. The strategy I will employ as I work towards my goals needs my attention.

Much like this stretch of the hike, I feel the strong urge to speed up my progress towards my new career. I'm no longer content with the slow steady pace that has brought me to where I am. I now want to run and take a big leap. Just what the leap will look like will be determined in my planning and strategy. Or maybe I'll have the opportunity to just follow my heart and it will be bold and unpredictable, just like the decision that led me to the Education degree program. Either way, the strings that once bound me to convention and expectation are broken and I feel free to choose.

WE MAKE THE WAY BY WALKING: SPIRITUAL PILGRIMAGE AND
TRANSFORMATIVE LEARNING WHILE WALKING THE CAMINO DE SANTIAGO –
BY ELIZABETH J. TISDELL, PROFESSOR OF ADULT EDUCATION, PENN STATE
UNIVERSITY HARRISBURG

*It is December 1, 2013, the first Sunday of Advent, a marker day of the season
of new beginnings. I sit here in my study where I write, surrounded by pictures
of my transformative experience of walking the nearly 500-mile pilgrimage
route of the Camino de Santiago from Southern France, over the Pyrenees, then
across Northern Spain to Santiago. I've written about it many times before,
but every time I do so it's as if I'm beginning again. How fitting that today,
the opening reading for Advent, this season of new beginnings, is from Isaiah
2, which says "Come, let as climb the Lord's mountain...let us walk in the
light of the Lord"! It's as if I'm climbing the Pyrenees yet again! It's as if I'm
walking along, capturing for the first time the wonder of the incredible mystery
of how the sunflowers turn their beautiful yellow faces toward the light—in
the light. They almost become the light, beckoning me along my Camino way.
I begin again this first Advent day. I re-member, re-write, re-live my Camino
experience. I make my way by walking, and experience once again the wonder
of chasing the light, the wonder of being chased BY the Light! "Come let us
walk in the Light..."*

I wrote these words this morning at 5AM, in my journal to the light of the fire
warming my cold study and one single purple candle. This was part of my meditation,
for the opening of Advent. I knew that today I needed to be writing this chapter, so
my experience of walking the Camino de Santiago was on my mind. Yet it is fitting
indeed that it somewhat spontaneously became part of my Advent meditation, as the
Camino experience continues to transform me. Exactly how it did so in the summer
of 2012 and continues to do so now is the subject of this chapter. Yet, somehow
words will never do justice or capture the experience completely. Hence, I invite
the reader to get a more complete experience of how the experience unfolded by
having a look at my blog: www.libbycamino.tumblr.com which partially captures
the experience in both words and pictures.

I had heard about, read about the Camino de Santiago for years before I decided
to do it. I grew up Catholic, and while my spirituality is inspired by many spiritual
and religious traditions besides Catholicism and Christianity, the religious tradition
in which I grew up with its multiple mystical and sacred traditions, images, icons,
symbols, and spiritual pilgrimage traditions continues to be an inspiration. So when
a friend heard me talking about the Camino in early May of 2012, she suggested I do
it. I was still a bit disoriented from a divorce in late 2011, and because spirituality is
a major component of my life, a 500-mile hike, walking in the footsteps of holy men
and women seeking inspiration seemed like a great challenge and opportunity. Given
that the landmark adult education text by Myles Horton and Paulo Freire (1990), *We*

Make the Road by Walking, has deeply influenced my own life, I thought it fitting that I literally make the road by walking my way into a new way of being. I booked the ticket, and off I went on July 4.

The Camino de Santiago, is literally "The Way of St. James," and was originally a Catholic Christian Pilgrimage way across Northern Spain. St. James was one of the apostles of Jesus, who went to the Iberian Peninsula and was martyred there. His remains are buried at Santiago de Compostela in Galicia in the Northwest of Spain. There are many routes, but the most traditional and well traveled (and the one that I took) is the Camino Frances, which begins in St. Jean Pied de Port in the South of France, and runs to Santiago.

To prepare, not only did I need to get my 56-year old body into physical shape, but I also needed to ground my being. Given the centrality of a sense of the spiritual combined with the spiritual, I combined meditation time with long walks carrying a pack. The 7th beatitude of Jesus from the Sermon on the Mount (Matthew 5), "Blessed are the peace-makers," particularly Neil Douglas-Klotz's (1990) midrash on the passage, which he suggests translates to "Blessed are they who plant peace in every step" was a part of my "personal theoretical framework" that guided the walk itself. What would it mean to try to "plant peace in every step"? This was a major grounding point not only in my preparations, but also in the walk itself.

I didn't necessarily intend to have a transformative learning experience in the academic sense of how transformative learning is described in the literature; I'm not sure one can "plan" a transformative learning experience anyway. Rather, I was doing this spiritual pilgrimage to try to walk my way into a new sense of being, but what I actually experienced was far more powerful and transformative than words can really describe. I learned how to manage pain, and I also discovered from both a spiritual and cultural perspective, the incredible value of my knowledge of the Christian scriptures that I grew up with in my Irish-American Catholic family of origin. The story of the healing of the paralytic as told in John 5:8 and the injunction to "pick up your mat and walk" guided my meditation that led me in how to transform my pain into something more meaningful. Space limitations do not really allow me to do justice to this examination, so here I simply summarize the 10 most important things I learned.

First, is the importance of moving/walking and its connection to meditation. Human beings were not meant to sit in front of a computer screen; they are meant to move! I've had trouble with my back for years, but I carried a 20-pound pack for 472 miles, and never had one problem with my back (aside from being tired at the end of a walking day)! Moving and walking has a miraculous power to help heal the body and the spirit too, particularly when it is approached as a form of meditation on the present moment in every step. While I've always been pretty good about getting some exercise, I've learned something new about walking, and walking as meditation. I got a dog upon my return, and together we've continued this practice.

Second, I discovered a new understanding of hospitality. The hospitality on the Camino is nothing short of incredible. For the most part, those who live on the Camino route do everything possible to be welcoming, to be somewhat nurturing through food and shelter at a limited price (or for donation) and to help you find your way. While language can be a minimal barrier, I learned that there are ways to communicate beyond language or other limitations by embracing this notion of hospitality. It reminded me of the biblical concept of hospitality and the injunction to make the stranger welcome, a concept that appears to be embraced by most who live on the Camino route. This sense of hospitality generally carried over to the *peregrinos* (pilgrims) as well. There are of course a few bad apples in the bunch, but for the most part I will be contemplating the meaning of Camino hospitality for a long time!

Third, the Camino is a microcosm of life. The Camino is not an escape from one's life; rather it is a microcosm of life itself. I met all of myself on the Camino, including my anxiety as I prepared to go, moments of insecurity about my self-concept along the way, manifestations of the ways that I deal with, avoid, and negotiate conflict. I experienced through a friend issues related to dealing with death, so death was present on the Camino as well, and is part of life itself. I also re-met my laughing self in ways I hadn't experienced in a long time! I found out how I deal with pain in its newer manifestations. I re-discovered once again how connected I am to my cultural and Catholic religious roots, in how I make meaning of things. While it is a luxury to take five weeks away from one's work life to walk the Camino, it is not an escape from life itself. Indeed, we take ourselves with us everywhere we go! So I re-met all the wonders and foibles of myself in new ways.

Fourth, I discovered a new meaning of turning towards the light. There were fields of sunflowers on the Camino—and they each had their own unique heads and faces always turning toward the light—turning toward the sun. I have never seen so many sunflowers, but being immersed in the natural beauty of Southern France and Northern Spain and just being outside for five weeks, made me contemplate the beauty of nature, and what it means to turn toward the Light in new ways!

Fifth, and related to light, is the notion of shadows, which literally and figuratively took on new meaning on the Camino. I found myself studying the shadows throughout the day, and my own shadow, and how it changed with the sun's trace across the sky. I also studied some of my inner and more metaphorical shadows, and how they too manifest and change over time. I'll be working on this for a long time!

Sixth, is a new understanding of pain. I don't think it's possible to do the Camino without experiencing the reality of pain. I only met two people who had no blisters on the Camino. There were many others who had more serious problems than blisters, such as issues with joints, or tendonitis; some had to even quit. I was blister free for 11 days, so I thought I was blessed, and then it was my turn for blisters. Sometimes at the beginning of the day, the pain was nearly excruciating for the first 15 minutes. At these times I would meditate on the Gospel miracle story of Jesus healing the paralytic, and the injunction to "pick up your mat and walk". I found this really quite powerful because after 15 minutes of walking, the pain would get less and less. While it didn't go away completely, I found I could walk through it, and I walked 18 miles for a couple of days when my blisters were at their worst. Part of the miracle for me was believing I could walk through the pain, that I could pick up my mat and walk, and walk I DID! This has other implications for both physical and emotional pain.

Seventh, relates to the importance of blessing one's feet! Feet are a major topic of discussion on the Camino. I've never given my feet much thought prior to this experience, so I have a great new appreciation of my feet, and have been thanking them for carrying me the nearly 500 miles that I walked. This new sense of feet, has given me new reflection on the Isaiah passage, "How beautiful on the mountains are the feet of those who bring good news, who proclaim peace…" I am now taking time every day to thank my 58-year-old feet for the good work they do!

Eighth is the power of group singing. I have always found singing some of the world's sacred chants to be incredibly grounding and moving. For the second half of the Camino I hooked up with a group of folks that also sang some of these same chants. We didn't sing all the time, but we'd begin the day singing for about 15 minutes, and then folks would more or less walk alone; then we might reconnect and stop and sing a chant or two in little churches along the way. We'd revert to marching songs when the terrain was tough or we were really tired. We entered Santiago singing a Taize chant, *Jubilate Deo*, as a round in four parts. Several in the square even joined us. It was fun and inspirational, and ironically this same chant was sung at the Pilgrims' Mass in the Cathedral two hours later! Who knew???

Ninth relates to the ongoing connection to one's cultural and religious roots. One of the things I rediscovered is how connected I still am to my cultural background and Catholic roots. The religious aspect may be because the Camino de Santiago was traditionally a Catholic pilgrimage, and I knew the meaning of the various symbols that I encountered along the way. Whether or not I formally identify as "Catholic" at this point in my life isn't really important, but I find that I can often easily access what I experience as the spiritual domain through many (not all) traditionally Catholic symbols and rituals when they are conducted with meaning and reverence. This sense of spirituality has little to do with, and is very different from, the institutional politics of the Catholic Church and its hierarchy. In any case, I have come to view this sense of access to the spiritual through Catholic ritual, symbol, and music as a blessing of my Catholic background.

Tenth, we do indeed make the way by walking! I began this journey with a reflection on "we make the road by walking" that I borrowed from a book by two of my adult education heroes, Paulo Freire and Myles Horton. I found out later that they borrowed the phrase from the Spanish poem, *Caminante*, by Antonio Machado. The English translation of the poem is:

Walker, your footprint is your path and nothing else;

Walker, there is no path, the path is made by walking.

By walking you make the path, and when you look back,

You see the track where you should never walk again.

Walker, there is no path, only the wake in the sea.

The words are so fitting to my Camino experience that I can't help but wonder if this Spanish poet ever actually walked it himself.

In many ways, this was a guiding meditation throughout this journey. I do believe we make the way by walking, and I am making my way. I have learned in a new way—an embodied way—the meaning of that phrase. While the only path is the path that I make, I am honored and inspired by those who forged a path to discover the wake in the sea. That's why I walked and why I am walking still. Indeed, it was, and still is (as they say in Spain) a "Buen Camino!" And it goes on and on, step by step…

It has been 16 months since I completed the Camino walk itself. It was a journey that made me not only "critically reflect on my assumptions" as proponents of transformative learning advocate, but it was a journey where I revisited and embodied some elements of my Irish-American Roman Catholic background that have taken on an embodied and transformative importance, the injunction to "Pick up my mat and walk." I learned not only that we do indeed "make the road by walking" (literally and metaphorically). I also learned something about a sense of a spirituality related to the land and to nature that is so often lost in our computerized lives. I learned that while we can learn a lot from the literature about the nature of wisdom, we often ignore the wisdom of nature. We can do an academic study of wisdom, but real wisdom comes only from walking the journey of life and attending mindfully to the rhythms of nature, oneself, and others. I learned that I am still "walking" the Camino, in every season of New Beginnings, such as the one offered today on this First Day of Advent of 2013. I am learning of the power and wonder of night and day, of what it means to turn toward the light, to be chased by the light, to walk in the light. So I continue to make my way by walking, and to be chased by that Light.

COMMENTARY

Libby's story is explicitly related to spirituality and what she learned by taking a rigorous, physically demanding pilgrimage. Kelly's story at first glance doesn't appear to be spiritual in nature, but by looking deeper into her story it's easy to see that she too is seeking to make her life more meaningful and to make a difference in the world and a life qualitatively different than the one of luxury and ease to which she had been heading. Both of these women want to learn more about something larger than themselves, more meaningful, and to thereby to connect with the spiritual. Unlike other chapters, these stories are journeys undertaken intentionally, focused on fulfillment and learning in otherwise successful, positive life experiences.

It is interesting to consider when these two journeys of transformation began. It is tempting to think of a disorienting dilemma as something finite, as in an event that can be described in certain terms where firmly held assumptions are brought into question. Kelly, however, describes the start of her journey as part of her natural development when approaching 50. Those unintended, normal changes related to aging, and tied with the departure of an only child, set her onto the trail and started a time of exploration. Her journey became intentional, and she found a return to college to be "a space for exploration." Another event moved her from her rational search to a search of the heart. She continued redefining herself through dialogue and through actual experience. She told us about her kimono, and this metaphor enables her to talk about control and freedom, moving from rigidity to being able to breathe, and being able to break constraints that had previously limited her. The trip continued, and continues, as she redefines who she is and how she wants to spend her time. It is clear that she has chosen a "road less traveled," eschewing society's normal drumbeat for more and more in exchange for a life of contribution. Kelly's journey, as she relates it in this story, has no definite start or end, and she continues to hike a path leading toward a redefinition of herself.

Libby's physical journey has a specific start and end, with nearly 500 miles in between. It is not clear when her transformative learning experience began. Was it, like Kelly, a natural part of her progression? Was it a continuation of her spirituality related to her Catholic Christian experience? Spirituality is clearly a key part of Libby's life, both professionally and personally, and it was to be a key part of this journey as well, whether it was manifested through meditation or singing. Interestingly, but not surprisingly, pain became a powerful lens through which Libby viewed her transformative experience. Her inner journey, looking at light and shadows and connection to her roots, also contributed to her transformational experience. Finally, the importance of relationships in transformative learning is clear in her story, not only as support but also in the sense of community.

These two stories exemplify the complexity of transformative learning; transformative learning encompasses a variety of processes which may not be linear but more circular or perhaps like a spiral. These journeys, spiritual in nature and nurturing the soul, are integrated into other changes that occur in a person's life. Both Kelly and Libby immersed themselves into different situations—one going back to school, another physically inserting herself into an entirely new situation. These stories demonstrated that transformative learning can be generative, it is not always about healing but is sometimes about building and transcending.

DISCUSSION: STORIES AND TRANSFORMATIVE LEARNING

Surgeons must be very careful When they take the knife! Underneath their fine incisions Stirs the culprit – Life!

Dickinson & Wetzsteon, *The Collected Poems of Emily Dickinson*, 2003, p. 28

Somewhere in every conceptual framework and inside every case study are human beings, the "Life" as Emily Dickinson reminds us. Every day adult educators facilitate learning, sometimes transformative, with human beings, not with hypotheses, propositions, or models. Every day individual lives are transformed in a variety of ways. Over time the cumulative effect alters the larger world. The ten stories of real lives captured in the preceding chapters demonstrate actual—not theoretical, not conceptual—transformative learning powerfully and personally. One way to interpret these stories is by exploring similarities. This chapter discusses the stories in relation to transformative learning theory. The interpretations we make are not the only way of understanding the stories; readers may find different ways of understanding the stories that apply more specifically to their research or practice or lives. We use these to start the discussion. Adult educators may use them or others when working with adult learners and we have some questions at the end of each one for reflection and engagement.

As readers, we are always delighted to find a story embedded in an article or a book chapter—a story that illustrates some facet of transformative learning. For example, MacKeracher (2012) tells her personal story to illustrate the role of experience in transformative learning in her chapter in *The Handbook of Transformative Learning*. And Clark (2012) weaves her story of a hip replacement surgery and her relationship with "Daisy" (her new hip) in a chapter on transformation as embodied narrative in the same volume.

As readers, we are always touched to find a story in which we find ourselves embedded, where we can see our story reflected, when we resonate with another's experience, and that opens our emotions, thoughts, and intuitions to possibilities otherwise off-limits or unimagined. For example, I (Michael) connected with Libby's story as I am on a spiritual journey myself. When Alyssa spoke of her mother I thought of my own mother and how the transformation of her own identity, started through my dad's decline and continuing through his death, was cut short prematurely and quickly through lung cancer after over 60 years of smoking. Adult educators can use stories to connect immediately with adults in ways that other learning experiences cannot.

We connect to others' experiences. Every adult experiences death, hope, despair, loss, and birth. Relationships, going to school, and traumatic events are part of the lives of many. Scholars look for themes by sorting through reams of data, but just about everyone also names the stories of their lives informally. Ask any adult about stories that have occurred through a lifetime and answers will range from "the boyfriend era" to the "time we were desperately poor" to the "exploration period." People connect with each other through stories. As we reflected upon these ten stories we identified ways of enhancing our understanding of transformative learning.

COLLECTING THE STORIES

When we began this project, we did not have a formal plan for collecting stories. We knew that transformative learning is a part of the human experience and so stories would not be hard to find. In fact, many times when either of us shared the idea of this book with someone, that person would tell us their story of transformation. In our practice as adult educators, we also routinely and regularly hear stories of transformative learning from our participants. So stories were not hard to find.

We realized that well written, illustrative stories of around 2,000 words would be more challenging to obtain. We decided that we would actively seek stories from within our own circle of relationships, looking for a range of experience but without trying to illustrate every context in which transformative learning occurs. Several of the stories came from students or former students, others from professional relationships. The result was the ten stories in this book. We worked with the authors to clarify the stories and did some minor editing, but the stories in the book are in the words of the authors.

Developing Chapter Categories

We had to decide how to group the stories into chapters. When we proposed the book we had a draft outline of possible chapters we thought might be key topics. These topics were developed by considering where transformative learning often occurs in our experience and in part through stories in the literature, such as in the *Handbook of Transformative Learning* (Taylor & Cranton, 2012). That informed our thinking as we gathered stories but did not constrain us. Sometimes when asking a person where to find stories the person offered a personal one of their own. That was always a meaningful and welcome surprise.

THE STORIES WE WERE TOLD

In our chapters we illustrate many of the contexts within which transformative learning occurs. When reading and discussing the stories, adult educators and learners will doubtless find more and alternative interpretations.

Formation and Transformation

From its inception, transformative learning theory has been considered an adult learning theory. The formation of values, beliefs, and assumptions most often happens in childhood, and the transformation of those values, beliefs, and assumptions in adulthood. Deep transformative learning cannot occur until something has formed that can be transformed. Individuals uncritically assimilate beliefs about themselves and the world at early ages (Gould, 1978). They are adopted as received, unquestioned knowledge (Belenky, 1997) from parents, teachers, community members, and other significant figures in their lives. In the case of one's identity, as the stories of Art, Jose, and Nayoung demonstrate, that means that significant identity change is not possible until a sense of "who I am" is developed in early years.

Jose, for example, developed the belief early in his life that he was not competent or smart. He had been forced to attend a "good" school following the closure of a school near where he lived, and in this "good school," the other students laughed at him. The process of changing identity—the transformative learning experience—continued through his completion of his degree in psychology and his master's degree and, even now, Jose writes that his journey has just begun.

Sung's transformation, as told by Nayoung, who interacted with him regularly as a student in her non-profit educational organization, began when at the age of sixteen he reconnected with his mother, who had disappeared when he was nine years old and left him alone and in dire straits. It continued at twenty as Nayoung, though her work at the school, helped him to consider his beliefs about himself and the world and he pursued his dream of becoming a teacher.

Art, as a young boy, made the decision to pursue education instead of working as a laborer in the fields, music, or drug dealing after observing a knife fight in a public square. That moment set his direction, which culminated in a successful personal and professional life. That, however, was not enough, and he decided to leave his thriving career. He "jumped into a void" where he found time for activities he found pleasurable. Music, which he loved as a child, became a part of his life again, along with painting, travel, and writing. His perspective about work changed, as he realized "life was not work, work was not life" and that a life of work was not most of life. This was a natural evolution as he rediscovered and began to reintegrate some of what was meaningful to him as a child. A financial crisis reframed his life perspective again, and survival became critical. The view of his future changed again, this time abruptly.

At what age are people capable of significant personal transformative learning? Sung, Art, Jose, and all of our storytellers developed perspectives about themselves as children that began changing in later years and then continued to develop. Sung began this process as early as the age of sixteen. Gould (1978) identified the ages of 16-50 as when the Evolution of Consciousness occurs. It is a time, he says, when people "come to be owners of our own selves." There is no clear age dimension as to when transformative learning can occur. Mezirow (2000, 2012) sees metacognition as an essential process in transformative learning, and metacognition is usually considered to be an adult cognitive process. However, other theorists of transformative learning (Dirkx, 2006) do not place cognition of any kind at the center of the theory. The question about how early transformative learning can occur would be a good question to test assumptions about transformative learning in a classroom or learning activity. As transformative learning theory evolves that is a question that will no doubt continue to be asked.

TRAUMATIC EVENTS

The popular book, *When Bad Things Happen to Good People*, by Harold Kushner (2001) reminds readers, many of whom have doubtless suffered tragedy themselves and are trying to deal with it, that traumatic events that can and do happen to anyone. Traumatic events shake up beliefs about oneself and the larger world. Kushner, a Rabbi who had spent most of his life helping other people believe in God, found himself reconsidering all that he had been taught about God after the tragic loss of his son because of a degenerative disease.

The stories of Susan, Laurence, and Mike demonstrate how a traumatic event can initiate profound re-assessment and then adaptation to the new reality. Susan and Laurence both found their lives changed irrevocably as a result of a dramatic physical change to their bodies. Mike went to the war in Iraq and "life was not the same" when he came back.

At some point, traumatic events are likely to touch most people and those they know. Few will have to deal directly with the shattering reality that Susan faced or the memories of war that Mike carries or the scary fall and subsequent diagnosis Laurence experienced. Each had to explore and to learn in order to adapt to their new worlds. It took Laurence a long time to discover that changing his eating habits would enable him to live without the symptoms of Meniere's disease. Susan's spinal cord injury caused her to have to learn not only how to walk but how to deal with others' perceptions of her and how she would approach life positively. These are dramatic examples of how people learn how to live with and adapt to new realities. They are also dramatic examples of how individuals transform their perspectives on who they are and go about looking at life through a different lens. Not all traumatic events are as dramatic as those presented here; readers may have experienced life-changing events that others would not find traumatic.

Transformative learning can be initiated by traumatic, often unexpected events. Why do some people—such as Susan, Laurence, and Mike—transform in positive, productive ways to learn and others do not? Are there personality traits that make one better able to deal with adversity? Are there factors in the environment that enable some people to develop more open and inclusive beliefs about the world while others become more narrow-minded and bitter? These are questions that these stories can evoke for adult learners and educators.

Optimism and Hope

Why is it that some people feel helpless in the face of difficult events while others respond with optimism? Martin Seligman discovered that some people develop what he called "learned helplessness," which is the belief that no matter what one tries it will not work (Peterson, Maier, & Seligman 1993). When that happens people give up. Seligman was also one of the founders of the positive psychology movement, a rapidly growing field of study and, his book, *Learned Optimism* (1998), describes how a person can be taught to be optimistic.

Mezirow says that disorienting dilemmas lead to self-examination with feelings of fear, anger, guilt, and shame and the questioning of assumptions. Does there then need to be a time of optimism and hope to then be able to move toward more, instead of less, open perspectives? Susan's story illustrates this. Another person after breaking her back might have given up, become bitter, or blamed the world for her situation. This was not how Susan approached her new challenges. As time passed, "a beautiful change began," and she saw her injury as a key part of her development. She described the choice she made as one of two paths, with her at the fork of the road. On one side was her past, and there was no going back to it. On the other side lay the future. She viewed that path as one with new learning opportunities and many unknowns. At that point she says she felt energized, hopeful, and eager.

Art had built a successful life for himself and voluntarily decided to change to a healthier, fulfilling life, and he so left his job and the life of work behind. Just four months later he found all his money frozen. He felt helpless, frightened, and adrift. He felt sorry for himself, and he remembered others he had known in his childhood town who had never attempted to leave. They remained downtrodden and content with their circumstances while Art had escaped to a better life. He did not want to be like that so he began to build his life again after financial struggle.

Susan and Art have dramatic stories of turning potentially negative situations into positive ones, looking forward to hopeful futures, but others in our book also have taken a positive approach under differing circumstances. Kelly and Libby, for example, are both on positive learning journeys. All have or have developed a sense of agency—personal power—which gives them hope and a belief that they have the ability to change their lives for the better. What differentiates people who deal with major loss with hope and optimism from those who approach it with pessimism or despair? Are having these two qualities an important part of the transformative learning process?

Jose emerges from a difficult family situation, years in prison, and a seemingly hopeless outlook for his future with optimism, hope, and the motivation to change his life. He gives back to other ex-gang members, guides others out of a life of chaos and destruction, activities that keep him grounded and motivated to get more out of life.

The Webs of Death and Loss

Loss, whether it be of our physical abilities, as we saw with Susan, the wealth we had counted on for our futures, as we saw with Art, or the sudden disappearance of a mother, as we saw with Sung, can be debilitating. For a very young boy, as Sung was, it can be devastating and leave a lasting imprint on his psyche which could only be lessened by reconnecting to the person he had lost.

As with any specific event, death may or may not result in transformative learning for those who are left behind, depending on the individual and his or her context and circumstances. As in all transformative learning, it depends on whether death results in a jarring of existing assumptions that leads to subsequent revision of those assumptions. Alyssa, a loving daughter to a father who died, came in to her own when she spoke at her father's funeral. He was a man she loved dearly and admired greatly. For her mother, this man was a husband now gone. Alyssa tells us of the transformation her mother experienced as she found open doors and new activities with a close group of friends in her life, but her basic identity, the identify that was interwoven with her husband, did not change. Alyssa's story illustrates the web of consequences that exist when a person dies.

Laurence lost salt. It does not seem like much when writing it but the voyage to be-a-person-who-does-not-eat-salt was a tortured one, starting with the day he fell for no reason, going through the uncertainty of not knowing when and where he would fall again, seeing doctors, discovering that he had either a life-ending tumor or an incurable disease, running serendipitously into a doctor who shared some hallway talk about a possible solution, to his decision to stop eating salt and finishing with the cessation of his symptoms of vertigo. Or was it? The real transformation continued after he stopped eating salt. Although it does not sound like a shift in identity, Laurence's experience extended to all of his eating habits and those of his family. He saw himself as a different person. The mind-body connection became real to him and he recognized that food choices had, in his case, substantial influence over the use of his body. And further, he observed how people knowingly sacrifice their health for a dubious pleasure when they do not have to do that.

Laurence lost salt, and salt had been one piece of a larger web of assumptions and beliefs about eating habits in Laurence's life. The salt seems minor, but from Laurence's perspective it was not. It was a conscious choice he made to eliminate frightening and debilitating symptoms, but it was more than that. He and his family changed the way they lived and ate, and in doing so Laurence changed the way he saw himself.

The question of whether transformative learning necessarily involves identity change is an interesting one. Individuals can experience the death of those they love without it being transformative. If death has a transformative influence long after it has occurred, and identity may remain essentially the same even after transformative learning occurs, then in what other ways might transformative learning experiences be differentiated? At what point is change of frame of reference, habit of mind, or meaning scheme deemed significant enough to be called transformative?

Educational Experiences

Just last fall I (Michael) spent a semester in Torino, Italy. I was there for three months and the experience was life changing, as I have written earlier. It is easy to assume that those who immerse themselves in different cultures through educational experience abroad will go through a transformative experience that will change the way they think and act for the rest of their lives (Graham & Crawford, 2012). They may be taking different classes than they normally would, meeting people who speak different languages and who have had very different experiences than they have had, and encountering different arts, cultures, religions, and businesses than they have before.

The same can occur on a university campus, where individuals meet people with different political beliefs than those they were brought up with, learn about whole new bodies of knowledge they didn't know existed, and are less tied to the social norms of their communities and families. It is no different in community college Adult Basic Education classes, where people nudge up against different ways of thinking, types of individuals, and have access to knowledge and shared information that can be disorienting.

Nayoung's project for North Koreans living in South Korea embodies adult learning principles. Students learn from each other in a supportive environment with a mentor present. The sessions are intended to meet very real needs of the students. Nayoung herself had to reflect upon her own perspectives as she built the curriculum.

A good part of Jose's story involved formal education. Although the process of transformation began with an epiphany about his ability to make choices while listening to a lecture while in a program at county jail, the transformation evolved from his interaction with teachers. Jose hated school, dreaded being called on by the teacher, and assimilated the assumption that he was not a "good student" in the "good school" he was forced to attend as a child. It took Jose some time to overcome this assumption, a time that was marked by years in prison, drug addiction, and generally, a sense of powerlessness and hopelessness. He heard a lecture while he was in a program in prison that was his first turning point, and he met a teacher and mentor in his first college experience who believed in him and changed his life.

Kelly's transformation began as she re-evaluated her life at the age of fifty while at the same time her son left for college. She decided to fill the vacuum in her life with something new and significant and that led her back to college, volunteering as a GED tutor, and other lectures and learning experiences outside her program. Along the way she changed in significant ways and she is now pursuing another master's degree where she will learn the skills necessary to make the meaningful contributions she now sees as important.

Educational experiences can be transformational as the stories Kelly, Jose, and Nayoung demonstrate, or they may not. Adult educators can facilitate opportunities for transformative learning. What do these stories suggest might need to be in place for transformation to be initiated?

Relationships

The importance of relationships to transformative learning occurs in several of the stories. Art had the support of his wife; Jose's wife stood by him and supported him throughout his difficult journey; Olutoyin's organization provides a supportive community for victims of abuse and to teach prevention; Mike's family also experienced war, and understanding their journey helped him to imagine a future "that is not completely damned."

Taylor and Snyder (2012), in their review of transformative learning research from 2006-2010, identify the role of relationships as becoming increasingly recognized as a significant part of the process of transformation. Relationships can change during a transformative process, they can provide support, and trusting relationships make it possible to have significant discussions for questioning and building understanding.

Jose's wife waited patiently for him, visited him every week while he was in prison, and never judged him. Jose describes his wife as his "anchor." He writes, "She was all that I had left. So from that point on, I decided that if I could not change for my own well-being, then I was going to do it for her." Jose also benefited from his relationship with a teacher and mentor who believed in giving people a second chance.

Nayoung's work as director of curriculum and content development for a special project for 80 North Korean students living in South Korea and her story of Sung's transformation is another example of the importance of relationships. Her mentoring sessions dealing with academic and life skills resulted in student reports of "eye popping" learning moments and shifting worldviews. Students shared each other's stories and learned what had impacted each other's lives. Sung participated as well in what must have been a powerful learning experience shared with the others.

Sung's story itself revolves around relationships, and in particular the relationship with his mother. With his father dying when Sung was young and then his mother abandoning him soon after, going so far as to destroy all traces of her in the house, Sung was left "to face the cruelty of life of severe hunger and poverty." He lived for seven years as a nomadic beggar and when Nayoung asked him to describe the one thing that kept him choosing life during those years he said it was that every day he thought about his mother, with feelings of hatred and betrayal, and that he had to stay alive to one day find out why she had left them. Reconnecting with her when he was 16 and finding out that his mother actually had the best of intentions for the way she left began a new, transformed relationship and also the transformation of Sung.

Sometimes, a relationship can be transformative, and the supporting person may not even know her or his impact on the learner. Sometimes the transformation occurs for both people involved, sometimes not. What are the varieties of ways relationship can influence transformative learning? Are relationships always important in transformative learning?

Social Change

Social change has a long history as a goal of adult education in general. The Highlander Folk School in Tennessee and the Antigonish Movement in Nova Scotia attest to this. Early theorists in adult education focused on social change, though this gave way to a humanist philosophy in the late 1970s and 1980s. Now, in the second decade of the 2000s, there is a return to critical theory and social change in our field.

Among the stories we collected, it is Olutoyin's story, Mike's story, and Nayoung's story that most clearly reflect social change as a central concept. Olutoyin describes the founding of WARSHE (Women Against Rape and Sexual Harassment) in her country (Nigeria). She worked with women to help them understand the nature of the oppression of women at the hands of religious leaders, men in general, and cultural norms in her country. She illustrates her work with the story of a woman seeking shelter from abuse through WARSHE and the response of a man to the work that WARSHE was doing. Olutoyin works tirelessly to make a change in the lives of women in her country.

Mike went to Iraq and returned as a different person. He didn't know where his life was going or how to cope with it. He returned to school, but he still struggled. But what Mike did was to turn his focus onto helping others in the same situation as he was in. He now runs veterans' groups, encourages narrative and storytelling as a way of healing for veterans, and speaks to groups about the need for support of veterans. He is working hard to make social changes that support the healing of veterans.

Nayoung works for a non-profit educational organization in South Korea as a director of curriculum and content development for a special project to 80 adolescent North Korean students living in South Korea. The North Korean learners have gone through extreme experiences during their life in North Korea and their journey to South Korea. Nayoung's goal is to foster social change among those students whose experiences were traumatic, difficult and oppressive.

Societal progress seems a worthy goal of adult learning in general and transformative learning specifically. But should social change be an expectation for educators facilitating transformative learning experiences or is that presumptuous? Are there times when educators should have a social change agenda in mind as an outcome for learners? Does social change via transformative learning need to be large scale or can it be as intimate as one person helping another person to read, as Kelly now does?

The Role of Adult Educators

It is interesting that Kelly and Mike became adult educators as a result of their transformative learning journey. Jose joined an organization that helps and guides ex-gang members, created a tutoring program for at-risk students, and volunteers for programs like the Family Literacy program that teaches English to immigrant and refugee parents. Kelly began tutoring adult GED students. On the other hand, starting as a political activist and union organizer, Olutoyin was already a university adult educator when she founded WARSHE. She was committed to social change using adult education strategies and then became the founder of an educational organization. Following his experience, Mike now facilitates learning for veterans. Perhaps there is something about transformative learning that draws people who have been through deep personal change to help others through a change.

We spoke of the role of relationships above and adult educators are always in relationship with adult learners. Sometimes that relationship can be very close, through small group or one-on-one sessions, some can be more distant. Some learners, as with Jose and Sung, have the benefit of professional teachers. Some adult educators, like Olutoyin and Nayoung, have profound effects on their students.

The qualities of adult educators who have facilitated transformative learning in this book are easy to discern. Caring is perhaps the most evident. Olutoyin founded an entire organization (WARSHE) because she cared so much about the victims of sexual violence. The Nigerian-based organization is over 15 years old and has given over 150 programs and documented over 70 cases of sexual violence and abuse and gender-based violence.

Nayoung, in her story, exudes caring. Just by observing how closely she listened to Sung's story and genuinely cares about his future it is easy to see that she is a caring educator. As in the case of Olutoyin, some adult educators go beyond facilitating learning to become advocates. Her goal is not simply transformative learning but extends to helping Nigerian women to become free of oppression, and as described above, has been actively involved in community activities. Olutoyin has gone so far as to write a book of stories about oppression. Are there other qualities of adult educators who facilitate transformative learning can be observed in these stories?

A Journey

We discussed the journeys of Libby and Kelly in Chapter 8, but in a sense, all transformative learning is a journey from one place to another. Sometimes the journey is tumultuous. Sometimes the path is unclear. Seldom is the way well lit at the beginning. Sometimes there are guides. Sometimes there are not. Sometimes it is a short trip to the grocery store, sometimes it is a saga. In every case the sojourners develop a more complete, more inclusive, and more informed view of the world and of themselves. The terrain might be rocky and destinations seem out of reach, but the traveler moves forward nonetheless.

It seems natural to describe a journey in exciting terms. Travelers are, after all, going to places where they have never been, to see sights they have never seen, and to experience life in ways they never would have otherwise. Unlike a physical trip, however, individuals undergoing personal transformation can never go back. Once something is known it cannot be unknown. Once something is seen it cannot have been unseen. Whether dragged out onto the road of transformation, like Susan was, or whether stepping out packed and prepared for the journey, as Libby and Kelly seem to be, one can never go home again.

Libby intentionally undertook her journey, physically, emotionally, and cognitively. Kelly used the metaphor of the trail as she described a normal disquiet that she proactively addressed by going back to school and volunteer. She may eventually change careers or not, but she is on the road of personal transformation. Both seem to be on journeys of adventure.

In considering transformative learning as a journey, how can adult educators prepare students for the trip? What inventory should be taken along? What skills developed to climb the mountains and to find nourishment along the way? Some of what adult learners might take include skills for self-reflection, relationships to carry the load, and an inquiring mind. Just the prior knowledge of how transformative learning occurs can take some of the fear away when it starts. Encouraging students to regularly test assumptions, to seek new perspectives and to try out-of-the-normal experiences will lower the risk of having reified, secure assumptions blown out of the water, thus initiating a traumatic life changing experience that could have been avoided or mitigated with better scouting ahead.

Developing Agency

The stories in this book involve people developing a sense of agency or personal power, through the transformative learning process. Laurence took control of his life by deciding to stop eating salt. Susan decided to make her disability into a plus. Mike looked for answers and teaches veterans. Olutoyin spends her life helping others develop agency through transformative learning. Jose took charge of his life by moving away from an unhealthy social environment, enrolling in community college and then continuing on to complete a bachelor's and then a master's degree, and by volunteering to help others in a number of ways. Libby took the initiative to go on a long, painful walk. Kelly decided to go back to school, twice. Art left a workaholic lifestyle to pursue other interests that were brewing inside, and then he took charge of his life again when he lost his financial security. After re-establishing a relationship with his mother, Sung is trying to go to school.

Transformative learning experiences often begin with a feeling that one has lost control and that the events of the world are sweeping them up. As one goes through the process individuals begin to reassert themselves into actively taking on and learning new roles until finally integrating into a more realistic view. If learners do not develop a sense of agency is transformative learning likely or even possible? How did educators in these stories help learners to build a sense of personal power?

SUMMARY

In this chapter, we engage in a discussion of the transformative learning stories presented in Chapters 4 through 8. We originally categorized the stories into the chapters according to similarities in the context and circumstances of the stories, but in this chapter, we wanted to go deeper into the commonalities across the stories. We wanted to highlight those aspects of the stories that might resonate with readers and to raise questions that might persuade readers to explore transformative learning stories of their own.

In this discussion, we write about formation and transformation with the understanding that individuals form values and beliefs uncritically in childhood and then question those values and beliefs in adulthood when they encounter events that call their original beliefs into question. We write about traumatic events, what Mezirow has sometimes called disorienting dilemmas—those events that transport us into questioning what we believe. And then, the idea of optimism and hope came up in the stories—people who could have been devastated by an event, but instead turned it into a positive learning experience. Death and loss, of course, is often associated with transformative learning, and we describe examples of this from our stories. Alyssa's story is especially interesting in this respect as it contains multiple layers. We all hope that educational experiences can be transformative.

Relationships seem to be central to many transformative learning experiences. This is not well addressed in the literature, but it comes through clearly in our stories. And it also comes through clearly in our experiences in practice. Social change adult education has a long history. In the stories we gathered, we see three examples of educators working toward social change as transformative learning (Olutoyin, Mike, and Nayoung). This takes us into the role of adult educators in fostering transformative learning and to how transformative learning is a journey, or a developmental path. And finally, and perhaps this is an umbrella for our discussion, developing agency (finding one's voice, standing up for oneself) is an important way of understanding the stories we have had the honor to present.

WHAT WE HAVE LEARNED

The sole purpose of human existence is to kindle a light in the darkness of mere being.

C. G. Jung, *Memories, Dreams and Reflections,* 1961, p. 326

The primary purpose of this book was not to add to the theoretical knowledge about transformative learning; nor was the purpose to conduct research on transformative learning. But in collecting and "listening to" stories of individuals in a variety of contexts, we have certainly learned a great deal, and we hope readers will also learn a great deal. In this chapter we review what we have learned through the collection of the stories, writing the commentaries on the stories, and discussing the stories. Writing a book is a learning process. Even authors well-versed in the field about which they are writing learn more about the content than they knew previously, often discovering new sources of information that had not been previously considered, or reconsidering it in relation to their existing knowledge. The authors learn from those with whom they engage as part of the writing process. They learn from each other and learn how to work together as well. This was true for us.

Collecting stories was an interesting part of the process. We discussed in Chapter 9 how we went about doing that. Some of the learning came from our own dialogue about the stories we might want to include in the book and the possibilities that emerged as participants presented their ideas for stories. The interaction with authors contributed greatly to our sense of the book. We adjusted and re-adjusted our way of organizing the stories, and this process shaped our thinking about storytelling and transformative learning in general.

So, it is clear that we have learned a great deal from the participants who contributed their stories. They gave a part of their lives to all of us so we may understand and learn from them. As anyone knows who has tried to write about themselves, and especially for others to read, the writing itself fosters self-reflection for the writer, and we appreciate this reflective stance in the stories. Then, as we considered how each story was transformative and further asked how stories fit with other stories, we learned more. Part of that constructed knowledge is represented in Chapter 9, where we considered what the stories seemed to tell us, and another part is represented here in Chapter 10. For example, we now understand more profoundly the importance of storytelling in describing and understanding transformative learning. We see how stories bring out the common characteristics in transformative learning across contexts (and therefore, demonstrate a way we can move to a more integrative theory of transformative learning). And we have seen how relationships are central to transformative learning in the stories we collected.

The literature on the process of transformative learning tends to emphasize a fairly standard series of steps or stages. Even though the theoretical literature has expanded beyond Mezirow's initial presentation of the theory, the published research (as presented in the *Journal of Transformative Education* and the *Adult Education Quarterly,* among other journals) tends to suggest that transformation is structured according to a linear and cognitive step-by-step process. What we have learned from the stories we collected for this volume is that there are other ways of experiencing transformative learning. Sometimes the seeds of the process exist in childhood and gradually flower in adulthood; other times transformative learning is deliberately sought out with no clear evidence of a "disorienting dilemma." Transformative learning is often dependent on relationships with others, perhaps especially the support of others. We learned, for example, how this was manifested in contexts where adult educators were supporting and helping others to learn and transform.

From the point of view of writing this volume, we learned how to work together, which is always a process of sorting out roles and responsibilities for co-authors and, importantly, of developing an understanding of where each person can make a particular contribution. As one example, after a discussion of ideas, Patricia often provided an advance organizer, sorting through the possibilities and suggesting an outline or a plan of work. This chapter began with a short list of ideas Patricia started and that we iteratively added to between us until we felt we had a complete list. Patricia then put together a draft outline which served to organize the writing of the first draft of the chapter.

STORYTELLING AND TRANSFORMATIVE LEARNING

Sometimes it is easier to write or talk about ourselves through stories. We both teach online classes and have found that the opportunity for students to write stories, examples, and express views often results in far deeper sharing than might be found in face-to-face situations. There is something about writing a story that will be read by people who are not sitting in the same room as we are that is conducive to a deeper kind of storytelling. It is rather like sitting on a long airplane trip with an interesting seat mate, one who is interested in our story, and a person who we will not face tomorrow morning in the office. As our students often say, "there's no one looking at me in the face, and I can write the story I want to write, and still get comments and feedback from others." Almost always, these stories lead to further reflection, insights, and emotional reactions.

Transformative learning stories share characteristics across contexts, but every story is different, just as every person is unique. Although we, as the authors of this book, shared many similar reactions to the stories, we also had different interpretations, which we worked through together, sometimes achieving consensus and sometimes not. Different people relate in different ways to different stories told by different storytellers; the attributes of transformative learning transcend stories.

Transformative learning stories can be filled with hope and optimism rather than being a negative disorienting dilemma. The stories in the book reaffirmed for us that the longstanding assertion that disorienting dilemmas result in traumatic feelings like guilt or anger does not encompass the range of positive emotions that might occur.

Transformative learning stories very often involve relationships with others. Those relationships can take a variety of forms—supportive, challenging, or negative. The relationships might range from intimate to distant, personal to professional, and directive to spontaneous and intuitive.

IMPLICATIONS FOR PRACTICE

Telling transformative learning stories in adult educators' practice has the potential to powerfully engage learners in transformative learning theory and their personal transformation. This we already knew from personal experience and the literature, yet we have learned to appreciate the value of storytelling even more than we did previously. Storytelling draws on learners' experiences, an important element of adult learning, and can facilitate collaborative inquiry and self-reflection.

It may be problematic or at least questionable for educators to interpret learners' stories rather than to let them stand as they were told (see Chapter 2). In two cases the storytellers found some differences in what they intended and how we interpreted their stories. Each learning situation is unique and adult educators should also consider whether inserting themselves between the story and the reader or listener detracts or adds to the learning experience. Better yet, educators can discuss this issue with learners, for example: What kind of commentary (if any) do you want from me, as educator? What kind of commentary (if any) do you want from your peers in this course? What should we do with the stories? How shall we treat them?

I (Patricia) have often incorporated fiction and storytelling in my practice. I even taught a special elective called "Transformative Learning through Fiction" in an adult education doctoral program. This course used a collection of Canadian short stories as the text. But our work on this book, and the way we collected and worked with participants' stories led me to take a different approach in a course I am currently teaching—a course called "Imagination, Authenticity, and Individuation in Transformative Learning." I introduced a forum in which students could write a poem, a short story, or describe and critique a short story written by someone else. Nearly all of the participants chose to write a short story. Some of these stories were fiction, but many were what might be called "creative non-fiction;" that is, they were stories of events in the participants' lives. I was surprised and pleased at the way in which our work on storytelling and transformative learning came so easily to life in my course.

IMPLICATIONS FOR THEORY DEVELOPMENT

As we have discussed previously (see Chapter 1), transformative learning theory has both benefitted from the development of various lines of inquiry and suffered from a fragmentation of perspectives. Scholars have spent a considerable amount of time and effort classifying the different kinds of transformative learning theory. After nearly four decades, it seems that it is time to return to work toward an integrative theory (Gunnlaugson, 2008). Mezirow's original theory illustrated an integrative approach to understanding transformative learning (he called on cognitive psychology, depth psychology, sociology, and philosophy in his development of the theory). The critiques of Mezirow's theory have led to a fragmentation of transformative learning theory, as writers have promoted one perspective over the others. Our work with stories in this volume illustrates one way that an integrative theory of transformative learning can be promoted. The stories we collected come from a variety of contexts and they describe quite different processes, but they have common characteristics. Also, within one story there is often more than one perspective on transformative learning theory. The perspectives co-exist in the stories. A holistic view is what we need to strive for in theory development.

Following this same line of thought, the stories in this volume call into question that transformative learning is, or can be, primarily cognitive in nature, or, for that matter, primarily intuitive and emotional. All stories contain cognitive processes and intuitive or emotional processes. The stories take us into the passion and drama of transformative learning. The stories are filled with hope and optimism in addition to more negative disorienting dilemmas. As we have mentioned, transformative learning theory has continued to rely on Mezirow's (1978) stages; these stages are helpful and have guided us for quite some time, but perhaps there are no stages, or perhaps there are processes that transcend the stages, or reorder them, or integrate them.

IMPLICATIONS FOR RESEARCH

Narrative inquiry is relatively new research methodology in education (and the social sciences in general) that brings participants' stories to the forefront of data collection. The research of Tyler and Swartz (2012) illustrates how this can work in the study of transformative learning. Research using fiction (Hoggan & Cranton, 2014; Jarvis, 2012) illustrates the same kind of process. In Hoggan and Cranton's study, for example, participants were 131 undergraduate and graduate students from two universities in the United States. Participants responded to a short story written by one of the authors (Chad Hoggan). Participants indicated that the story promoted change, fostered reflection, connected with personal experiences, and engaged with emotions.

As I (Patricia) was writing this description, I had the CBC radio on in the background, and I caught the words, "narrative" and "identity" and "storytelling" in the conversation in the program. Human beings have always been storytellers; stories shape our identities. Bill Randall, from St. Thomas University in New Brunswick, Canada, is speaking as I write. Randall is known for his work in gerontology and storytelling, and also for his work in how we "re-story" our lives over time. I am thinking that there is a very interesting area for future research in this area. And then, I thought about a doctoral student whom I advised who did his dissertation on the stories that the terminally ill have to tell (Sauers, 2012). I have never read such moving stories, and Michael Sauers made sense of these stories in a way that has the potential to contribute to the practice of all caregivers of the terminally ill.

We do not know if the theory will ever lend itself to extended quantitative research, scales, and instruments but perhaps the possibility has not been explored enough yet to know. Transformative learning research to date has been mostly qualitative in nature. But, there are some forays into quantitative approaches. King's (2009) survey on transformative learning has been used extensively as a way of selecting participants who have engaged in transformative learning—participants who are then interviewed. Cranton, Stuckey, and Taylor (2013) have completed a careful process of survey development related to the outcomes and processes of transformative learning in which they have established construct validity through expert review, content validity, and reliability in a pilot study with 136 participants ranging in age from 24 to 64 years.

What We Learned from Each Other

We have learned from each other through the process of writing this book. We have also learned about each other and developed a personal relationship though we have only met once, when presenting at the same session at a transformative learning conference years ago. We have never spoken through writing this book, yet we know considerably more about each other as people now, and such matters as our love for dogs and books and the impact of winters in New Brunswick, Canada and Boise, Idaho.

In my (Michael's) case, I have been able to develop more depth of knowledge about transformative learning than I had before, and I particularly learned from Patricia, who has been a thought leader and author in the field for many years. My more simplistic knowledge of transformative learning is now more nuanced, complex, and informed. I understand much better the depth of transformation that transformative learning theory requires. By knowing more, I also realize how much I do not know. There is a hubris one develops about one's own beliefs and this process, as I wrote above, has given me the opportunity to critically reflect on my own assumptions about transformative learning. That has been humbling for me, and something I consider to be a very positive learning experience.

Not only did I (Michael) learn much about the content of transformative learning from Patricia, I also learned quite a lot about how to write a book from her; she was always generous and, as importantly, often simply modelled how to do it well.

105

As co-authors, we had different approaches to writing. Patricia is more linear in thinking and writing; Michael is more intuitive. Michael's approach is eclectic and jumbled and time consuming, often started by tossing ideas around in his head before taking an approach, and he seldom knows exactly what he will write about until the keyboard starts clicking. Fortunately, Patricia has a structured approach that provides scaffolding for his work and always has a good grasp of what she intends to write. We each learned from the other's writing style.

I (Patricia) learned from Michael how to let go of my linear and structured approach to writing in order to appreciate and take advantage of Michael's intuitive and creative way of understanding the concepts we were writing about. And perhaps even more importantly, I was coaxed into considering perspectives on transformative learning that I had rejected (for example, that younger people can engage in transformative learning).

Part of our own discussions about the "voice" of this book included deliberating about how personal we should make it. In other words, we asked ourselves how much of our "first person" selves and our personal stories we should integrate into it. Though we found third person objectivity to be foundational, we decided that it was important that we model storytelling ourselves, so that readers could see us subjectively and personally.

We also have different backgrounds related to transformative learning and our careers in general, with Patricia focusing more on higher education and Michael more on human resource development. We were able to contribute different examples and contexts to the writing and learn from each other in this way.

SUMMARY

Our goal with this book was to present stories told in the voice of the individual, without scholarly citations and concepts separating the writer from the direct experience. We hope that this will result in a more direct connection between the reader and the story. For us, when students or other people we know tell personal stories there often is almost immediate resonance. We respond not just on an intellectual level but also emotionally, spiritually, and even physically.

Our interpretations of the stories are informed by our knowledge and experience and thus are limited. Others will interpret them in different ways or disagree with our views. Our stories are socially constructed, and our interpretation of others' stories is also socially constructed; that is, there is no one truth, or at least no truth that can be completely comprehended, but rather many ways of understanding. We hope to make the case for more permeable, less distorted perspectives about transformative learning by connecting directly with individual transformative experience.

In this chapter, we describe what we have learned from the stories we collected. We go on to discuss implications of our work with stories for practice, theory, and research. We finish with what we have learned from each other.

We both have a strong belief that transformative learning has the potential to improve lives and society, often powerfully. There are few other areas of education that can connect so intimately with our humanity and can contribute to self, mutual, and societal understanding. Stories are a portal to understanding transformative learning and to understanding ourselves and others. We are privileged to be a conduit between the stories in this book and those who will read them.

REFERENCES

Apps, J. W. (1996). *Teaching from the heart.* Malabar, FL: Krieger.

Bandura, A. (1997). *Self-efficacy: The exercise of control.* New York, NY: W.H. Freeman.

Barker, J. A. (1985). *Discovering the future: The business of paradigms.* St. Paul, MN: ILI Press.

Belenky, M. F. (1997). *Women's ways of knowing: The development of self, voice, and mind* (10th anniversary ed.). New York, NY: Basic Books.

Belenky, M. F., & Stanton, A. (2000). Inequality, development, and connected knowing. In J. Mezirow & Associates (Eds.), *Learning as transformation: Critical perspectives on a theory in progress* (pp. 71–102). San Francisco: Jossey-Bass.

Boje, D. (2001). *Narrative methods for organizational and communication research.* Thousand Oaks, CA: Sage.

Boje, D. (2006). Breaking out of narrative's prison: Improper story in a storytelling organization. *Storytelling, Self, Society: An Interdisciplinary Journal of Storytelling Studies, 2*(2), 28–49.

Boje, D. (2007). *Storytelling organizations.* London: Sage.

Boje, D., & Tyler, J. A. (2009). Story and narrative noticing: Work alcoholism and authoethnographies, *Journal of Business Ethics, 84,* 173–194.

Boorstin, D. J. (1983). *The discoverers* (1st ed.). New York, NY: Random House.

Boyd, R. D. (1985). Trust in groups: The great mother and transformative education. In L. S. Walker (Ed.), *Proceedings of the Annual Midwest Research-to-Practice Conference in Adult and Continuing Education.* Ann Arbor: University of Michigan.

Boyd, R. D. (1989). Facilitating personal transformation in small groups. *Small Group Behavior, 20*(4), 459–474.

Boyd, R. D. (1991). *Personal transformation in small groups: A Jungian perspective.* London: Routledge.

Boyd, R. D., & Myers, J. B. (1988). Transformative education. *International Journal of Lifelong Education, 7,* 261–284.

Bradley, M. Z. (1982). *The mists of Avalon.* New York, NY: Knopf.

Brookfield, S. (1990). *The skillful teacher: On technique, trust, and responsiveness in the classroom* (1st ed.). San Francisco, CA: Jossey-Bass.

Burns, J. M. (2003). *Transforming leadership: A new pursuit of happiness.* New York, NY: Atlantic Monthly Press.

Campbell, J. (1972). *The hero with a thousand faces.* Princeton, NJ: Princeton University Press.

Campbell, J., & Moyers, B. D. (1988). *The power of myth* (1st ed.). New York, NY: Doubleday.

Carson, R. (1964). *Silent spring* (1st Fawcett Crest ed.). New York, NY: Fawcett Crest.

Charaniya, N. K. (2012). Cultural-spiritual perspective of transformative learning. In E. Taylor & P. Cranton (Eds.) *Handbook of transformative learning* (pp. 231–244). San Francisco, CA: Jossey-Bass.

Clark, M. C. (2012). Transformation as embodied narrative. In E. Taylor & P. Cranton (Eds.) *The handbook of transformative learning: Theory, research, and practice* (pp. 425–438). San Francisco, CA: Jossey-Bass.

Clark, M. C., & Rossiter, M. (2008). Narrative learning in adulthood. In S. B. Merrian (Ed.) *Third update on adult learning* (pp. 61–70). New Directions for Adult and Continuing Education, no. 119. San Francisco, CA: Jossey-Bass.

Cranton, P. (2006). *Understanding and promoting transformative learning* (2nd ed.). San Francisco, CA: Jossey-Bass.

Cranton, P. (2012). Reflection through fiction. *Educational Reflective Practices, 1*(2), 21–34.

Cranton, P., & Carusetta, E. (2004). Developing authenticity in teaching as transformative learning. *Journal of Transformative Education 2*(4), 276–293.

Cranton, P., & Roy, M. (2003) When the bottom falls out of the bucket: A holistic perspective on transformative learning. *Journal of Transformative Education 1*(2), 86–98.

REFERENCES

Cranton, P., & Taylor, E. (2012a). Transformative learning theory – Seeking a more integral theory. In E. Taylor & P. Cranton (Eds.) *The handbook of transformative learning: Theory, research, and practice* (pp. 3–20). San Francisco, CA: Jossey-Bass.

Cranton, P., & Taylor, E. (2012b). Transformative learning. In P. Jarvis (Ed.), *International handbook of learning* (pp. 194–201). Routledge Press.

Cranton, P., Stuckey, H., & Taylor, E.W. *Assessing transformative learning outcomes and processes.* Paper presented at the 10th International Transformative Learning Conference, Meridian University, Petaluma CA.

Daloz, L. A. (1986). *Effective teaching and mentoring.* San Francisco, CA: Jossey-Bass.

Dante, A., & Ciardi, J. (2003). *The divine comedy: The inferno, the purgatorio, and the paradiso.* New York, NY: New American Library.

Denning, S. (2005).*The leader's guide to storytelling: Mastering the art and discipline of business narrative.* San Francisco: Jossey-Bass.

Dickinson, E., & Wetzsteon, R. (2003). *The collected poems of Emily Dickinson.* New York, NY: Barnes & Noble Classics.

Dirkx, J. (2000). After the burning bush: Transformative learning as imaginative engagement with everyday experience. In C. A. Wiessner, S. Meyer, & D. Fuller (Eds.). *Challenges of practice: Transformative learning in action.* Proceedings of the Third International Conference on Transformative Learning. Teachers College, Columbia University.

Dirkx, J. (2001). Images, transformative learning, and the work of soul. *Adult Learning, 12*(3), 15–16.

Dirkx, J. (2006). Engaging emotions in adult learning: A Jungian perspective on emotion and transformative learning. In E. W. Taylor (Ed.), *Teaching for change: Fostering transformative learning in the classroom* (pp. 15–26). New Directions for Adult and Continuing Education (no. 109). San Francisco, CA: Jossey-Bass.

Dirkx, J. M., Mezirow, J., & Cranton, P. (2006). Musings and reflections on the meaning, context, and process of transformative learning: A dialogue between John M. Dirkx and Jack Mezirow. *Journal of Transformative Education, 4*(2), 123–139.

Dominice, P. (2000). *Learning from our lives: Using educational biographies with adults.* San Francisco, CA: Jossey-Bass.

Douglas-Klotz, N. (1990). *Prayers of the cosmos.* San Francisco, CA: Harper

FitzPatrick, S. (2005). Open-ended tangled hierarchies: Zen koans and paradox in public administration. *International Journal of Public Administration, 28*(11/12), 957–971.

Freire, P. (1993). *Pedagogy of the oppressed* (New rev. 20th-Anniversary ed.). New York, NY: Continuum.

Frost, R. (1946). *The poems of Robert Frost.* New York, NY: Modern Library.

Gaston, W. (1994). *The Cameraman.* Macmillan Canada.

Glen, J. M. (1996). *Highlander: No ordinary school* (2nd ed.). Knoxville: University of Tennessee Press.

Gould, R. L. (1978). *Transformations: Growth and change in adult life.* New York, NY: Simon and Schuster.

Graham, N., & Crawford, P. (2012). Instructor-led engagement and immersion programs: Transformative experiences of study abroad, *Journal of Higher Education Outreach and Engagement, 16*(3), 107–110.

Gunnlaugson, O. (2008). Metatheoretical prospects for the field of transformative learning. *Journal of Transformative Education, 6*(2), 124–135.

Habermas, J. (1971). *Knowledge and human interests.* Boston: Beacon Press.

Hall, E. T. (1973). *The silent language.* Oxford England: Anchor.

Hoggan, C., & Cranton, P. (2014, in presss). Fiction, learning and transformation: A report on research. *Journal of Transformative Education.*

Horton, J. (2013). Teaching science through story. [Article]. *Teaching Science: The Journal of the Australian Science Teachers Association, 59*(3), 38.

Horton, M., & Freire, P. (1990). *We make the road by walking.* Philadelphia: Temple Univ. Press Press.

Jackson, S., & Holmes, A. M. (2005). *The lottery and other stories.* Penquin.

Jarvis, C. (2006). Using fiction for transformative learning. In E. W. Taylor (Ed.), *Teaching for change: Fostering transformative learning in the classroom* (pp. 69–78). New Directions for Adult and Continuing Education, no. 109. San Francisco, CA: Jossey-Bass.

110

Jarvis, C. (2012). Fiction and film and transformative learning. In E. W. Taylor & P. Cranton (Eds.), *The handbook of transformative learning: Theory, research, and practice* (pp. 486–502). San Francisco, CA: Jossey-Bass.

Jarvis, P. (2008). *Religious experience: Learning and meaning, Transformation (02653788)*, pp. 65–72. Retrieved from http://ida.lib.uidaho.edu:2048/login?url=http://search.ebscohost.com/login.aspx?dire ct=true&db=aph&AN=31177021&site=ehost-live&scope=site

Jung, C. G. (1971, Originally published in 1921). *Psychological Types*. Princeton: Princeton University Press.

Kasworm, C. E., & Bowles, T. A. (2012). Transformative learning in the workplace: Leading learning for self and organizational change. In E. W. Taylor & P. Cranton (Eds.), *The handbook of transformative learning: Theory, research, and practice* (pp. 388–407). San Francisco, CA: Jossey-Bass.

Kegan, R. (2000). What 'form' transforms? A constructive-developmental approach to transformative learning. In J. Mezirow & Associates (Eds.), *Learning as transformation: Critical perspectives on theory in progress* (pp. 35–70). San Francisco, CA: Jossey-Bass.

Kenyon, G., & Randall, W. (1997). *Restorying our lives: Personal growth through autobiographical reflection.* Westport, CT: Praeger.

King, K. (2009). *The handbook of the evolving research of transformative learning based on the learning activities survey.* United States: Information Age Publishing, Inc.

King, S. (2009). *Under the dome.* Scribner.

Kiteley, B. (2005). *The 3 a.m. epiphany: Uncommon writing exercises that transform your fiction.* Cincinnati, Ohio: Writer's Digest Books.

Knowles, M. S. (1975). *Self-directed learning: A guide for learners and teachers.* Chicago: Follet.

Knowles, M. S. (1980). *The modern practice of adult education.* New York, NY: Association Press.

Kuhn, T. S. (1962). *The structure of scientific revolutions.* Chicago: University of Chicago Press.

Kushner, H. S. (2001). *When bad things happen to good people* (20th anniversary ed.). New York, NY: Schocken Books.

Lamb, N. (2008). *The art and craft of storytelling: A comprehensive guide to classic writing techniques.* Cincinnati, Ohio: Writer's Digest Books.

Lawrence, R. P. (2012). Transformative learning through artistic expression: Getting out of our heads. In E. W. Taylor & P. Cranton (Eds.), *The handbook of transformative learning: Theory, research, and practice* (pp. 471–485). San Francisco, CA: Jossey-Bass.

MacKeracher, D. (2012). The role of experience in transformative learning. In E. W. Taylor & P. Cranton (Eds.), *The handbook of transformative learning: Theory, research, and practice* (pp. 342–354). San Francisco, CA: Jossey-Bass.

Mandela, N. (1994). *Long walk to freedom: The autobiography of Nelson Mandela* (1st ed.). Boston: Little, Brown.

Meijiuni, O. (2012). *Women and power: Education, religion, and identity.* Ibadam, Nigeria: University Press.

Merriam, S. B., & Kim, S. (2012). Studying transformative learning: What methodology? In E. W. Taylor and J. Mezirow (Eds.), *Transformative learning in practice: Insights from community, workplace, and higher Education* (pp. 56–72). San Francisco, CA: Jossey-Bass.

Meyer, S. R. (2009). Promoting personal empowerment with women in East Harlem through journaling and coaching. In E. W. Taylor and J. Mezirow (Eds.), *Transformative learning in practice: Insights from community, workplace, and higher education* (pp. 216–226). San Francisco, CA: Jossey-Bass.

Mezirow, J. (1975). *Education for perspectives transformation: Women's reentry programs in community colleges.* New York: Center for Adult Education, Teachers College, Columbia University.

Mezirow, J. (1978). Perspective transformation. *Adult Education, 28,* 100–110.

Mezirow, J. (1991). *Transformative dimensions of adult learning.* San Francisco: Jossey-Bass.

Mezirow, J. (2000). Learning to think like an adult. In J. Mezirow & Associates (Eds.), *Learning as transformation: Critical perspectives on a theory in progress.* San Francisco, CA: Jossey-Bass.

Mezirow, J. (2012). Learning to think like an adult. In E. W. Taylor and J. Mezirow (Eds.), *Transformative learning in practice: Insights from community, workplace, and higher Education* (pp. 216–226). San Francisco, CA: Jossey-Bass.

Mezirow, J., & Associates (1990) (Eds.). *Fostering critical reflection in adulthood: A guide to transformative and emancipatory learning.* San Francisco, CA: Jossey-Bass.

REFERENCES

Millay, E. S. V. (1972). *Letters of Edna St. Vincent Millay*. A. R. Macdougall (Ed.). Westport, Conn: Greenwood Press.

Moore, T. (1992). *Care of the soul: A guide for cultivating depth and sacredness in everyday life*. New York, NY: HarperCollins.

Nelson, A. (2009). Storytelling and transformative learning. In B. Fisher-Yoshida, K. D. Geller, & S. A. Schapiro (Eds.), *Innovations in transformative learning: Space, culture, and the arts* (pp. 207–222). New York, NY: Peter Lang.

O'Sullivan, E. (2012). Deep transformation: Forging a planetary worldview. In E. W. Taylor & P. Cranton (Eds.), *The handbook of transformative learning: Theory, research, and practice* (pp. 162–177). San Francisco, CA: Jossey-Bass.

Orwell, G. (2008, first published in 1949). *Nineteen eighty-four* (1st Harvest ed.). Boston: Houghton Mifflin Harcourt.

Peterson, C., Maier, S. F., & Seligman, M. E. P. (1993). *Learned helplessness: A theory for the age of personal control*. New York, NY: Oxford University Press.

Rabin, C., & Smith, G. (2013). Teaching care ethics: Conceptual understandings and stories for learning. *Journal of Moral Education, 42*(2), 164–176.

Rogers, C. R. (1961). *On becoming a person; a therapist's view of psychotherapy*. Boston: Houghton Mifflin.

Rohr, R. (2003). *Everything belongs: The gift of contemplative prayer*. New York, NY: Crossroad.

Rohr, R. (2009). *The naked now: Learning to see as the mystics see*. New York, NY: Crossroad.

Rossiter, M., & Clark, M. C. (2007). *Narrative and the practice of adult education*. Malabar, FL: Krieger Publishers.

Sauers, M. (2012). *Storytelling by adults diagnosed with terminal illness: Narrative identifying through dialogical research*. Unpublished doctoral dissertation, Penn State University.

Seligman, M. E. P. (1990). *Learned optimism*. New York, NY: Pocket Books.

Seligman, M. E. P. (1998). *Learned optimism*. New York, NY: Pocket Books.

Selman, G. (1989). The enemies of adult education. *The Canadian Journal of University and Continuing Education, 15*(1), 68–81.

Sinclair, U. (1906). *The jungle*. New York: Doubleday, Page & Company.

Sloan, A. P. (1964). *My years with General Motors* (1st ed.). Garden City, NY: Doubleday.

Suler, J. R. (1989). Paradox in psychological transformations: The Zen koan and psychotherapy. *Psychologia: An International Journal of Psychology in the Orient, 32*(4), 221–229.

Taylor, E. W. (2008). Transformative learning theory. In S. B. Merriam (Ed.) *A third update on adult learning theory* (pp. 5–16). New Directions for Adult and Continuing Education, no. 119. San Francisco, CA: Jossey-Bass.

Taylor, E. W., & Cranton P. (Eds.). (2012). *The handbook of transformative learning: Theory, research, and practice*. San Francisco, CA: Jossey-Bass.

Taylor, E. W., & Snyder, M. J. (2012). A critical review of research on transformative learning theory, 2006–2012. In E. W. Taylor & P. Cranton (Eds.), *The handbook of transformative learning: Theory, research, and practice* (pp. 37–55). San Francisco, CA: Jossey-Bass.

Tennant, M. (2012). *The learning self: Understanding the potential for transformation*. San Francisco, CA: Jossey-Bass.

Tyler, J. A., & Swartz, A. L. (2012). Storytelling and transformative learning. In E. Taylor & P. Cranton (Eds.), *The Handbook of Transformative Learning: Theory, research, and practice* (pp. 455–470). San Francisco, CA: Jossey-Bass.

Tennant, M. (2012). *The learning self: Understanding the potential for transformation*. San Francisco, CA: Jossey-Bass.

Tolliver, D., & Tisdell, E. (2006). Engaging spirituality in the transformative higher education classroom. In E. W. Taylor (Ed.), *Teaching for change: Fostering transformative learning in the classroom* (pp. 37–48). New Directions for Adult and Continuing Education, no. 109. San Francisco, CA: Jossey-Bass.

Watts, A. (1989, originally published in 1957). *The way of Zen* (1st Vintage Books ed.). New York, NY: Vintage Books.

Whyte, D. (1994). *The heart aroused: Poetry and the preservation of the soul in corporate* America (1st ed.). New York, NY: Currency Doubleday.

Whyte, D. (2001). *Crossing the unknown sea: Work as a pilgrimage of identity.* New York, NY: Riverhead Books.

Zander, M. J. (2007). Tell me a story: The power of narrative in the practice of teaching art. *Studies in Art Education: A Journal of Issues and Research in Art Education, 48*(2), 189–203.

Zinsser, W. K. (2004). *Writing about your life: A journey into the past.* New York, NY: Marlowe.

Zinsser, W. K. (2006). *On writing well: the classic guide to writing nonfiction* (30th anniversary ed.). New York, NY: HarperCollins.

INDEX

CPSIA information can be obtained at www.ICGtesting.com
Printed in the USA
BVOW08s1701040215

385859BV00008B/29/P